A HISTORY OF CHARING

The parish from earliest times to 1900

A HISTORY OF CHARING

The parish from earliest times to 1900

By members of the
Charing and District Local History Society

Market Place Charing SDD 09

built on relationships

Kent
County
Council

Charing and District Local History Society

Published by

Charing and District Local History Society

Copyright © 2011 Charing and District Local History Society and the authors

ISBN 978-0-9570299-0-3

Printed in Great Britain by
Geerings, Ashford, Kent

Contents

Maps

List of Figures

List of Tables

Foreword

In 1984 the Charing and District Local History Society published a short book, under the auspices of the Kent County Library and Kent County Council, entitled *About Charing: Town and Parish*. It comprised twenty essays on a range of topics which collectively, in the words of the introduction to the book 'sought to keep alive the spirit of Charing Town and give glimpses of our parish which has far more to offer than a lovely setting, attractive buildings and a colourful history'.

Twenty-five years on only a handful of copies were left for sale and it was clear that something would have to be done to replace it. A reprint was not possible and in any case could not be done without updating aspects which had changed with time. The form of the book did not lend itself to revision and so the History Society committee decided to embark on a completely new book. A writing group of volunteers was formed. The aim was to produce a general history of the area from earliest recorded time showing how the place we now know as Charing came to be populated and how the inhabitants influenced the development of the land and buildings.

One of the contributors to the first book was Pat Winzar who at the time was a member of the History Society committee and secretary of the Kent County Local History Committee which eventually became the Kent History Federation. She served the Federation in every committee role and was its president from 2003-2009. She became chairman of the Charing society in 1985 and led it with skill and sensitivity for twenty-two years. Writing this book has been made easier by all the researches undertaken by her over many years. She has collected, transcribed and made available numerous documents dating from the Middle Ages to the mid eighteenth century. We have also been able to take advantage of her unpublished diploma thesis on trade in seventeenth-century Charing, and of her papers published in *Archaeologia Cantiana*.

Since the previous publication, further archaeological information has come to light, and the church, archbishop's palace and houses of the parish have been studied in considerable depth. At the same time, historians of Kent have published a great deal more on the history of the county generally which allows the story of Charing to be seen in a wider context.

In the past twenty-five years considerable change has occurred. A new housing complex has been built, many large gardens and open spaces have been in-filled, faces have come and gone but the spirit of Charing lives on and this book seeks to nurture and sustain it. I commend it to the reader and hope that it will give much pleasure.

Brian Easton
President, Charing and District Local History Society

Acknowledgements

Numerous members of the Charing and District Local History Society have been involved in the production of this book. First and foremost are the authors, Brian Easton, Peter Kidson, Sarah Pearson, Stephanie Reed and Pat Winzar, who have all worked hard on producing the text over the last eighteen months. Former members of the writing group who helped to shape the outline of the book in its early stages were Pat Thompson and Chris Williams. The volume was edited by Sarah Pearson.

Other members of the Society have contributed in various ways. The authors are grateful to Sidney Dray for drawing several Charing buildings, and for allowing us to publish some delightful Christmas card vignettes which can now be shared with a wider audience; to the Society's Photographic Group: Dorothy Burdick, Ray Selves, Cynthia Shaw and Harold Trill, who provided a number of early drawings and photographs, and to Tylden Reed who took other photographs. Ron Beale, Jill Leyland, Kate McIver, Alex Norris and John Voller read the text in draft and made valuable comments and corrections; Jill Leyland kindly copy edited the final product; Jackie Grebby undertook the onerous task of designing and laying out the book for the printers; and John Hogben for publicity and marketing prior to publication. Without their hard work and the financial support of the History Society committee, the authors would not have been able to publish this book.

The final result has also benefitted greatly from professional help with some illustrations: John Hills, of the Department of Geography and Life Sciences at Canterbury Christ Church University, drew the tailor-made maps inside the end covers on a Geographical Information System. Allan T Adams turned survey drawings of the church, palace and Vicarage Cottage into high-quality illustrations, and has allowed us to publish several of his sketches of Charing buildings.

Bridgett Jones, although not immediately involved in the production, has transcribed medieval Latin documents for the Society over many years, particularly material from the National Archives; this assistance has been invaluable. Tim Bain-Smith, Ken DaSilva-Hill, Elizabeth Ellen, the late Ian Gambrill, John Owen and Steve Salter have generously supplied information or allowed us to publish material they own. We are also grateful to the staff of the Centre of Kentish Studies at Maidstone and the Canterbury Cathedral Archives for supporting Society members with their research both now and in the past, and for permission to reproduce maps and plans in their safe keeping, to the Trustees of the Wheler Foundation for permission to publish the 1736 map of the Wheler estate in Charing, and to the Kent Archaeological Society for permission to reproduce the Charing villa plan from *Archaeologia Cantiana*. Every effort has been made to acknowledge the copyright holders of all illustrations produced in this book. The Society is also extremely grateful to Kent County Council and the Brett Group for generous grants to help cover the cost of publication.

Finally, no book on historic buildings could be written without the help of the owners, occupiers or guardians of the buildings concerned. Charing's church, palace and historic houses have been studied over many years, and the authors are indebted to all who have facilitated access and allowed surveys to be done and photographs taken. Without their help the last three chapters could not have been written. In particular Brenda Ansell, Peter Burton, Roy Cooper, Kevin Giles, Gail Greig, Peter Lunn, and Elizabeth and Stuart Whyte have assisted us in the recent past. Past or present, we thank them all for their contributions.

Aerial view of Charing village, c.1960 (S Salter)

Chapter 1: Charing before the Norman Conquest

by Peter Kidson

Charing before Charing

In 1801 when the first census was taken, the ecclesiastical parish of Charing covered 4,681 acres. The present civil parish is slightly larger (see Map 1), and the shape is not quite the same, but there is reason to think that the greater part of this piece of land was already a recognised historical entity when the name first appeared in the records a thousand years before the census. The parish is spread across a varied landscape that includes parts of the North Downs, the Vale of Holmesdale (the shallow valley to the south of the Downs), and the Greensand Ridge. The Downs are chalk, the Vale of Holmesdale is gault clay, and the greensand a mixture of limestone (Kentish Rag) and sandstone (Fig. 1.1). These strata were laid down towards the end of the Cretaceous geological period, perhaps seventy million years ago, that is to say within the last one per cent of cosmic time. In subsequent ages a ripple, caused by the earth's movements that produced the Alps, elevated the Weald to the south and depressed the Thames estuary to the north, and the present profile is the state to which the upland has been reduced by erosion over several million years.

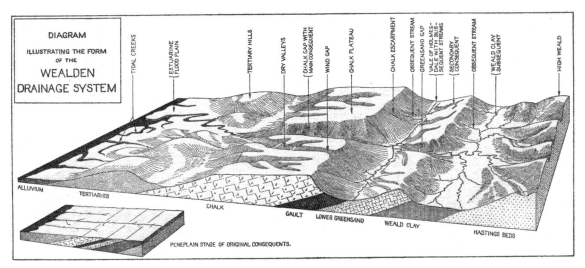

Fig. 1.1 Diagram of Kent's geology and drainage from the north coast to the high Weald (A G Ogilvie, Great Britain, Essays in Regional Geography, *Cambridge University Press, 1937, fig. 6)*

The surface soils lend themselves to vegetation ranging from woodland to scrub and grassland. Chalk is porous but the clay beneath it is impervious, so precipitation that does not drain off collects on the bedding plane at the base of the chalk where it forms a natural reservoir. Fed by this cistern, a series of streams break surface at the edge of the gault, and run south to augment the upper reaches of the river Stour, which flows eastward at the southern end of the parish along the Vale of Holmesdale towards Ashford, Canterbury and the sea. The spring line is where the village came to be located in due course, amid good farming land, and with wells and dew ponds to augment the rivulets, the water supply needed to sustain continuous human habitation has never been a problem. But there were no permanent settlements until long after the precursors of homo sapiens reached Britain, more than half a million years ago. Over ninety per cent of that long period was taken up by the several so-called stone ages, known chiefly through the flints shaped into rudimentary tools such as axe heads by which they can be chronologically classified. In a quarry at Swanscombe, no more than twenty-seven miles from Charing on the other side of the Downs, a particularly rich find of flints was accompanied by the skull of a hominum from a collateral branch of the anthropoid family who lived c.300,000 years ago. Flints are formed naturally in chalk, and anyone who got to Swanscombe is likely to have passed by Charing on the way, though nothing remotely that ancient has yet been found there. In fact, none of the stone ages are well represented in the archaeological evidence in Charing. The earliest meagre signs of human presence in the area are Mesolithic, i.e. post-glacial, flints from quarries in the greensand at the southern edge of the parish.

In effect, it was the retreat of the glaciers c.10,000 years ago that brought this long prelude to an end. Although Kent was beyond reach of the ice, it was left uninhabited for a long period during the Ice Age and the repopulation was a long, slow process. Conventionally divided into Mesolithic, Neolithic, Bronze and Iron Ages after the materials that respectively distinguish them, what really matters was the gradual replacement of hunting and gathering by subsistence farming, which led to a more settled lifestyle and fostered the development of social institutions in the form of religious rites and customs. But the discovery of how to obtain and use metals, which made agriculture possible, often involved trading over long distances. Commercial traffic came to be channelled along recognised trackways such as the North Downs Way (Pilgrims' Way) along and below the scarp of the Downs, or drove roads over the Downs towards the Weald. All of this had become well established in the ambience of Charing long before the Romans brought Britain into the age of recorded history, which was not all that long ago. Nearly everything that we are concerned with in this book happened within the last million days, i.e. since c.720BC.

The first information we have about Kentish society is in Julius Caesar's history of his Gallic wars, which included his two expeditions to Britain in 55 and 54BC. He tells us that the people who lived in the coastal areas known to him – i.e. Kent – were different from those further inland. They were quite recent arrivals from across the Channel who came as raiders but remained to become agrarian farmers. The population was dense and the settlements close together. They had bronze and gold coinage and iron, which was produced in the form of iron pieces of fixed weight. He mentions the names of four Kentish kings, though not the tribes over which they ruled – and he has much to say about their methods of warfare.

What does not appear in Caesar's account is perhaps no less interesting than what does, and the record can be amplified by archaeology. There were as yet no real towns in the county that Caesar could recognise as such, though Canterbury was perhaps developing in that direction, and the settlements were hardly villages. Some of them were fortified enclosures, but most of them were little more than self-supporting entities spread across the landscape. The vast majority of the early Iron-Age sites so far identified are concentrated in the east of the county, and it was only in the later stages that they appear in any number along the northern coastal strip or in the Vale of Holmesdale. It could be that this had something to do with the ability of the newcomers to plough the heavier soils of the deposits above and below the chalk, something to which Caesar seems to allude in his description. There is no certain evidence of Iron-Age sites in the vicinity of Charing before the Romans came: a short-lived settlement has been excavated in a gravel pit near the village, seemingly abandoned by AD100; a Roman farm building near Wickens at the eastern edge of the parish could indicate the whereabouts of an earlier settlement, and a single potin coin, minted *c.*25BC, has been found nearby on the Pilgrims' Way, all of which may, or may not, imply that the place was inhabited in the years that followed.

A hundred years after Caesar's punitive visit, the Romans returned to Britain, and this time they came to stay. The invasion met with little resistance. A decisive battle was fought at the Medway crossing which opened the way to the Thames fords and bridges; and so far as Kent was concerned, it was all over. The Charing area seems to have played no part in the campaign, and the Cantiaci, which was the Roman name for the people who lived in the canton or *civitas*, became docile provincials. As the part of the province of Britain that was closest to the continent, Kent was the gateway through which lines of communication passed connecting it with the rest of the Empire. In recent times the Vale of Holmesdale has become the principal conduit through which traffic with mainland Europe flows, and the prehistoric North Downs trackway and the so-called Pilgrims' Way, just north of Charing, have been seen as the ancient forerunners of this route. But the Romans did not see it that way. For them the main military highway was north of the Downs. The roads from the ports of entry – Richborough, Dover and Lympne – converged on Canterbury, and the rest of the road system spread out like capillaries from the main artery. The primary purpose of the major roads south of the Downs was to connect the iron works of the High Weald to centres of distribution for their principal customers, who were the military, i.e. to the north for the army, and to Dover and Lympne for the Channel fleet. The iron industry was based on the easily worked ironstone of the Wadhurst clay beds of the Weald; but smelting hearths have been found in the sand quarries near Charing, others near Wye, and there appear to have been a whole row of small-scale workings on the edge of the gault that made it worth paving a proper road parallel to the Pilgrims' Way to service them. A stretch of this road east of Lenham has recently been excavated, and signs of its existence have been identified east of Charing.

The roads and the iron works were directly connected with the military concerns that brought the Romans to Britain. What they were seeking was a permanently secure northern frontier. After giving up thoughts of pressing eastward into Germany, Augustus decreed that this should be the Rhine, but, as Caesar had realised, a powerful independent Britain could pose a potential threat to the rear of that line, and it was to neutralise this danger once and for all that they occupied as much of the island as they thought necessary. They did not come to bring the benefits of Roman civilization to the natives, and a policy of Romanisation went no further than to make the occupation viable. Very few Romans from Rome came to Britain, a vernacular form of Latin did not replace the Celtic language, and it was left to Britons to adopt as much of a Roman life-style as they thought fit – in rural Kent the established pattern of the pre-Roman Iron Age continued much as before, with its close connections with northern France and Belgium.

The little farm building near Wickens excavated in 1975 might almost have been designed to illustrate these affiliations (Fig. 1.2). It was a simple building, perhaps erected in stages as its functions changed, but in its final form the plan bore a striking resemblance to a similar farm building in the Gallo-Roman villa ensemble at Anthée near Namur in Belgium. Virtually the same length, with a similar arrangement of rooms and portico, the only notable difference was an extra attachment at Anthée. The Anthée ensemble was a vast affair, comprising a residential villa at one end of an open court *c.*500m long, with no less than twenty subsidiary buildings strung out around it, one of which resembled the plan at Charing. No one would suggest that there was anything on the scale of Anthée at Charing, but a modest operation with a villa and one or two outbuildings would satisfy the evidence. There were no signs that the Charing building was ever lived in, so the analogy implies that there ought to have been accommodation for the work force and a residential villa somewhere in the vicinity. As yet no trace of either has been found, though hopes of identifying the whereabouts of the villa have not been given up. This could be important in view of what happened later.

The end of Roman rule and the occupation of Kent by the Teutonic invaders who settled there is anything but clear. The nearest thing to a contemporary account, written in the sixth century by a Celtic monk, Gildas, was more like a saga than a chronicle of events. Bede, who up to a point is trustworthy, was writing three hundred years after the event, by which time the distorting effect of a long historical perspective was unavoidable. It was Bede who called the Kentish settlers Jutes, a name that has given rise to much debate about where they came from. But the important thing about the Jutes is not what they called themselves when they arrived but that they soon came to be known as the *Cantware*, i.e. their own version of the Roman *Cantiaci*, which suggests that they positively wanted to be assimilated. For obvious reasons they converged on the fertile farm lands, and the genetic evidence seems to show that they mingled with, rather than replaced, the indigenous population. If that is what happened it is unlikely that established tenure patterns were wiped out and a completely new set of property boundaries put in their place, all of which leads one to wonder whether a Romano-British estate in the Charing area might not have passed more or less intact into their hands.

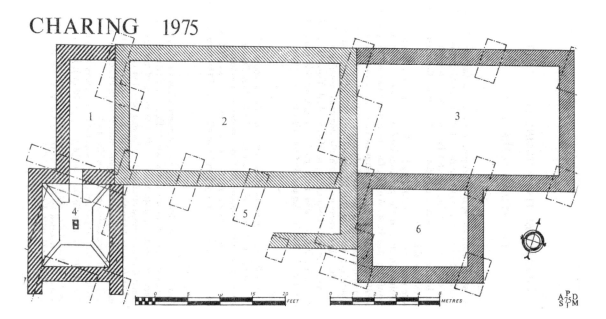

Fig. 1.2 A Romano-British building in Charing. Phase 1: rooms 2 and 5; Phase 2: rooms 1 and 4; Phase 3: rooms 3 and 6. The dashed lines indicate the areas excavated (A P Detsicas, 'A Romano-British building in Charing', Archaeologia Cantiana, *vol. 91, 1975, p. 108)*

Charing before Domesday

It was not until *c.*450 years after the arrival of the Kentish Jutes that Charing was at last named in a surviving document. This was a charter dated 799 concerning lands that were acquired by the archbishop of Canterbury from Egbert II, king of Kent, *c.*780. Shortly afterwards, between *c.*785 and 796, when Offa, king of Mercia, was effectively overlord of Kent, these lands were confiscated, but after his death the archbishop persuaded his near successor Coenwulf, to restore them, and the charter was the legal endorsement of this transaction. In it, Charing, variously spelt, was said to be thirty *aratros* in extent (see 'Roman measures' box). From the brief description, and the circumstances that gave rise to it, we can form some ideas about the medieval origins of the place.

The name itself is singularly unhelpful. There are plenty of suggestions as to its meaning, but none more convincing than the rest. The description of the Charing part of the land returned to the archbishop in 799 may be more revealing. The literal meaning of the word *aratrum* was plough. More often than not the size of the Canterbury properties in Kent are given in sulungs, a term derived from the Latin *suleus*, a furrow. As measures, they both obviously referred to ploughland and they were almost certainly interchangeable. Like *jugerum*, however, the standard Roman unit of land measure which derived from *jugum*, a yoke, they were used to denote simply the size of a piece of land. In most of the country the name commonly used for this purpose was 'hide', and sulungs are often thought to have been the Kentish equivalent of hides. The definition of the hide seems to have been somewhat elastic, though in most parts of the country the norm seems to have been 120 acres. That may have been the case with sulungs in some places, but in one instance where we are given a specific equation – namely St Martin at Dover, which like Charing was listed in Domesday Monachorum as one of the minsters of Canterbury – we are told that '400 acres and a half make two and a half sulungs'. If the half meant half an acre and is ignored, it follows that one sulung would be 160 acres. If this definition is applied to the Charing sulungs, the estate would have been about 4,800 acres, which exceeds the area of the parish in 1801 by a mere 120 acres. However, a more likely reading is that the half meant half a hundred, in which case the equation would make the sulung 180 acres and the Charing estate 5,400. The 1801 parish would then have been just short of 7/8ths of the estate.

The affair which brought Charing above the horizon of recorded history can be seen as the manoeuvring of the last nominally independent kings of Kent, their overlord the king of Mercia, and the archbishop of Canterbury, who were engaged in a complicated power struggle. At the time in question Offa of Mercia, currently the most powerful ruler in the country, was trying to extinguish the last traces of Kentish independence. He needed to acquire lands in the kingdom, from which pressure could be put on the archbishop of Canterbury, in order to implement his grand design of setting up an independent Mercian archbishopric at Lichfield. After the battle of Otford in 776, which gave him a few years respite from Mercian interference, Egbert II of Kent sought to forestall these impending dangers by making over 'in perpetuity' to Canterbury a group of three properties totalling forty-four sulungs, of which Charing was thirty. The attempt misfired. Egbert acted through his minister, and after 785, when Offa was again in control of the situation, this gave him a legal loophole for revoking the endowment, which was put into loyal Mercian hands. In 787 at the Council of Chelsea, the archbishopric of Lichfield was established, and papal privilege was accorded to it. Understandably, Offa was *persona non grata* at Canterbury, but so long as he remained all powerful nothing could be done about it. However, as soon as he died in 796 his high-handed programme of Mercian aggrandisement fell apart. Lichfield soon reverted to suffragan status, and the archbishop was in a position to seek the recovery of his lost property. The charter of 799 was the record of his success, and the Charing estate remained a possession of the archbishopric until Cranmer surrendered it to Henry VIII. The episode was not only its debut in the annals of history, but the one and only occasion when Charing was at the centre of events of national importance.

It was a direct consequence of the Canterbury connection that Charing became a minster church of the cathedral. If there was a church before it became ecclesiastical property all evidence of it has disappeared. Minsters were semi-monastic establishments of priests, in effect flying squads of professional clergy, who could perform the liturgies that only ordained priests were empowered to do at churches in the recently converted areas within striking distance of the minster. It was a system that preceded the formation of parishes, designed so that bishops could keep a watchful eye on the situation lest there were lapses into paganism. The only detailed list that we have of the churches attached to the Canterbury minsters is in the late eleventh-century Domesday Monachorum, when these arrangements had been in existence for five hundred years, and were already giving way to the parochial pattern. Egerton is the only name given for a dependency of Charing, far fewer than for other minsters, which may mean that most of the client churches had severed their connections. But in the manuscript there is a gap after Egerton that could have been left to be filled in by the missing names and never was, so we shall never know the full story.

The siting of minsters has recently been a topic of interest among historians and archaeologists. Wherever possible they are thought to have been located at places that already had religious connotations; in Kent these were more often than not Romano-British, and that would add a distinctive nuance to the hypothesis that the Roman past of the villa had a religious aspect. The patron saints of the church at Charing are St Peter and St Paul. This was

Roman measures and their legacy in England

It is worth taking a closer look at the measurements in the 799 charter. It is extremely unlikely that an accurate survey would have come out as the exact number of an extremely large measure like a sulung, and even more improbable that a survey of any kind would have been made by anyone in Anglo-Saxon Kent. The only people who could, and did, measure land with any pretence of accuracy were Roman *agrimensores* (land surveyors), and the people who smoothed out their figures to nice round numbers were the Roman tax collectors. It is almost certain that what the charter of 799 called 30 *aratra* was based on a Roman assessment that had been remembered and translated into the areas used in Anglo-Saxon Kent.

It can be worked out how this was done. When the English acre was finally given its legal definition in a statute of Edward I, it was described as a strip of land 40 x 4 perches. The perch was a linear measure of 16½ English feet or 5.0292m. The word perch came from the Latin *pertica* – a measuring rod. Roman taxes were a kind of income tax, based on the profitability of land, which was measured by an assortment of *perticas* ranging from 10 to 17 Roman feet. The Roman foot was 0.296m so the 17ft *pertica* was 5.032m…, i.e. all but the same as the English perch. The smallest area used by the Romans was the *actus*,

a popular dedication, especially in Kent where there are no less than thirty-nine, second only to the Virgin. The first of these was at Canterbury itself, where the earliest and largest group of churches that formed the abbey of St Augustine's went under that denomination. This does not mean that Charing was in any sense a dependency of the abbey. Named together, Peter and Paul were in a special sense the saints of Rome, and the dedication would always insinuate that Charing was under the protective care of the spiritual headquarters of western Christendom. It may have done more than that. Ecclesiastics everywhere were constantly on the look out for signs of the presence of the faith, as far back as records go, and often beyond that. St Augustine's mission was sent from Rome with the express purpose of restoring and extending to the whole country the episcopal Church that had once existed in Roman Britain. Christian symbols have been found at Lullingstone villa in western Kent, and Lullingstone can hardly have been the only case of its kind. So it is perhaps not wholly irrelevant to wonder whether a Romano-British villa at Charing might have contained similar reminders that the people who once lived there had also been Christians. If there was something of that kind, it might help to explain why Charing became one of the archbishop's residences. As yet, of course, the whole villa argument is entirely circumstantial, but anyone who refuses to look beyond the little firm evidence that is available to what is no longer there will almost certainly get it wrong. The idea is at least worth bearing in mind.

The plan of the church that was presumably built soon after 799 should lie buried beneath the present building, for church sites seldom changed. Nothing is known about it, what damaging effects the Viking raids in Kent may have had, or whether it was rebuilt after the Norman Conquest as many were; but the aisleless nave of the Gothic church preserves one standard feature of Anglo-Saxon church design, and its dimensions could have been systematic enlargements of what was there before, which was a common way of conveying the sense of continuous identity through a series of renewals.

---

a square of 120 x 120 square feet, but this was inconveniently small, and surveys made do with the *jugerum*, which was defined as two *actus* of 120 x 240 = 28,800 square feet, or often as a square of 170 x 170 = 28,900 square feet. From this it can be shown that five English acres all but equalled eight square *jugera*.

In other words there was a fixed conversion ratio between the acre and the *jugerum*, and the Charing land in the 799 charter was almost certainly so many *jugera* before it was turned into acres and sulungs. This is a very good reason for thinking that it had once been a Romano-British villa estate. The reduction of large numbers of *jugera* to smaller numbers of bigger units was not something that the Anglo-Saxons are likely to have done. These were there when they arrived. It had to do with the need for food production on a commercial scale to feed the Roman armies stationed on the frontiers. This accounts for the huge villa estates in north-eastern France and Belgium, and Kent was probably part of the same operation. A Roman based system of measures in Britain was the most abiding of all the consequences of the Roman occupation, and it is through Kent that it passed to the rest of the country. The other measures that became standard, i.e. the foot, yard and fathom, were also Roman, of architectural origin, and probably arrived with St Augustine's mission as part of the equipment needed to design churches.

With the passage of time, as the Church integrated itself into Kentish society, the supervisory role of the minsters, which served their purpose very effectively while settlement was ongoing, ceased to have any relevance when boundaries between churches were stabilised and the principle of a resident for the church in each area was widely accepted. Minsters as such lost their separate ranking and became in effect parish churches like their dependents. We cannot say when this happened at Charing, but it was probably a fait accompli before the first of the post-Conquest archbishops, Lanfranc, reorganised the diocese.

The community that the church served cannot have numbered more than about 300. The other focal point was the manor house, or archbishop's palace as it much later came to be called. The manor itself was the archbishop's land, presumably the property that was returned to him in 799, though it acquired several detached additions at unspecified times. The manor was an economic unit. Part of it was the home farm attached to the manor house; the rest was let out on terms that could be rent or services, and which varied according to the legally defined status of the incumbents (see Chapter 2). The farmsteads were scattered over the landscape. There was no sign of the common land or strip farming of the Midland counties, nor as yet of anything that could be called a nucleated village, though where a drove road over the Downs to the Weald crossed the Roman road there was probably a cluster of dwellings for the staff that kept the manor house in working order. We have no idea how often the archbishop stayed at Charing but it was intermittent. There would be a reeve in regular residence, who attended to the financial affairs of the manor and as the archbishop's proxy discharged the judicial functions of the lord of the manor, according to the customs and laws of Kent, as these had been set down in writing by the seventh- and eighth-century kings when they were still independent rulers. The pre-Conquest set-up passed undisturbed into the new dispensation, and it is described in more detail in Chapter 2.

Like most manors, Charing sought to be self-sufficient and probably was. But unlike most manors, the Canterbury connections gave it a toehold of contact in a wider world, and for all we know the anonymity of its rural lifestyle was enlivened by occasional glimpses of the great names on the archbishop's guest list. It is doubtful whether the visitors ever noticed the locals.

Chapter 2: Medieval Charing

by Sarah Pearson

Domesday and later

From the time of the Norman Conquest evidence for Charing's history becomes more plentiful, starting in 1086 with the entry in Domesday Book. This was an inventory for taxation purposes of all the land in England, but it tells us who had held it before 1066, who held it in 1086, what it consisted of in terms of land and people, and what its value had been in 1066 and was in 1086. It was written in a sort of Latin shorthand that is anything but easy to understand. Charing is listed as a possession of the archbishop:

> The archbishop himself holds Charing in demesne. It is assessed at 8 sulungs. There is land for 40 ploughs. In demesne is 1 sulung, and there are 4½ ploughs. 26 villans with 27 bordars have 27 ploughs. There are 12 slaves, and 1 mill rendering 40d. There are 25 acres of meadow, and woodland for 26 pigs. In all it was worth £24 in the time of King Edward [i.e. before 1066]; when acquired as much; now it is valued at £34, and yet it renders £60.

It was not called a manor since the term was not used in the Kent Domesday, but that is what it was, and from the description we can obtain a picture of what it was like in the eleventh century. As discussed on p.5, the sulung was an area of land somewhere between 120 and 180 acres, which makes it hazardous to define the size of the manor precisely. In Charing seven sulungs were farmed by the tenants, and one eighth was in demesne, i.e. in the archbishop's hands, although we learn from Domesday Monachorum, a text related to Domesday, that it was actually worked by a 'farmer' or leaseholder, who paid £40 per annum to the archbishop plus an extra charge of 4 6s 1½d called *gabulum*.

The manor was not a discrete area of land, but somewhat more fragmented. The core may have been an enlarged version of the nineteenth-century ecclesiastical parish which is known from the tithe map of 1840 (Map 1), which extended into modern Egerton and Stalisfield parishes, as well as into the Weald. Pett was a separate estate of 80-100 acres, held by the archbishop but actually part of the manor of Little Chart. There was probably a village in the vicinity of the manor house, but most of the farming tenants, in particular the *villans*, are likely to have resided in dispersed holdings across the manor. From later documents we can be fairly certain that the arable land held by the archbishop himself was just to the north of the manor house, below the scarp of the Downs. The twenty-five acres of meadow were where the grass for hay grew best, probably near the Stour to the south of the parish. Some woodland was probably up on the Downs, but some was in outlying 'dens' in the Weald. This woodland, mostly oak and beech, was used for its timber and also for pasturing pigs. The twenty-six pigs mentioned were those which had to be supplied to the archbishop, who was owed one for every seven or ten kept by the tenants. Finally, there was a mill, to which the tenants presumably took their corn for grinding.

The sixty-five inhabitants mentioned in Domesday indicate the number of households in the manor. To these should be added William, who held Pett, and his four slaves. If we conjecture that there were four – five people per household, then the population would have

Fig.2.1 Map of the Wheler estate, 1736. This shows the demesne lands or home farm of the manor of Charing with the great Westcourt/Westfield and Eastcourt/Eastfield arable fields below the Downs to either side of the village (deposited at the Centre for Kentish Studies: Map U369/P3; © Trustees of the Wheler Foundation)

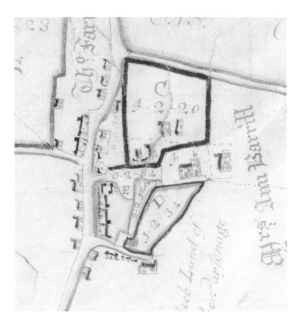

Fig.2.2 Detail of 1736 Wheler map, showing the church, palace ('C') and High Street. The triangle of land just west of 'C' is where The Swan Inn was later built, and 'E' is called Market Place in the key to the map (deposited at the Centre for Kentish Studies: Map U369/P3; © Trustees of the Wheler Foundation)

been between 280 and 350 people. There is much debate about their status. *Villans* were probably free tenants who were later known as *gavelkinders*. They paid a small rent and had to perform services for the lord, but were free to buy and sell their land. On average across Kent they formed around sixty per cent of tenants, although in Charing the percentage was rather less. *Bordars* were more strictly controlled and had more tasks to perform for the lord. Slaves as such were dying out by this date, and were probably akin to the later *cotlanders*, who had the most onerous tasks of all. These categories will be discussed later since their tasks were enumerated in the thirteenth century.

The value of the manor was evidently increasing during the eleventh century, rising from £24 to £34 in the space of twenty years, but it actually brought in as much as £60. Although the notional value to the crown was £34, the new Norman overlords, ultimately the king but beneath him the archbishop, made sure that their estates were run more efficiently than before the Conquest and got a larger return from their tenants than had previously been the case. Whether the tenants were also more prosperous is another matter altogether.

The practice of leasing the demesne is likely to have continued throughout the twelfth century. Charing actually has evidence of this in a lease granted to Adam of Charing between 1174 and 1182 which states that he was to have the 'farm' of the manor as both he and his father before him had had back to the time of Archbishop Ralph (1114-22). He was to pay the archbishop £32 per annum, plus £4 7s of *gabulum* which amounted to nearly £40 in total. The amount for the lease had changed, but the *gabulum*, whatever it was, was very much the same as it had been in the eleventh century.

The thirteenth century

This very legalistic picture of Charing, which is all we have in the eleventh century, can be filled out in the thirteenth, when the surviving documents are more informative. By this time the demesne land was no longer leased but managed directly by the archbishop's staff. In the time of Archbishop Kilwardby (1272-78), a list of receipts and expenditure for the year 1273/4 (written this way because at that time the year ran from 25 March to 25 March) tells us a great deal more about the organisation of the land, the manor house, and the local men who worked for the archbishop. The farm had steers, oxen, cows, cart horses and pigs. Produce from the manor was sold, and supplies of wheat, barley, rye and vetch were brought from the archbishop's manors of Boughton [under Blean] and Teynham, north of the Downs. Various payments are recorded from the tenants, and wages were paid to the bailiff (in overall charge of several manors), the reeve or serjeant (who managed the farm) and the beadle (who dealt with the tenants), as well as to a smith, a carpenter, a thatcher, two carters, a ploughman, a harrower, a shepherd and a haymaker. During the period of the accounts, various partitions were made and plastered in the manor house and in outbuildings such as the cowshed and pigsty. Thatching was undertaken on the almonry and gate, and on farm buildings such as the great barn, the hay barn, and the oxhouse. Work was going ahead on the watermill, and stallage was charged in the market. In other words the manor was a large and complex agricultural operation with a residential hub. There was clearly a settlement in close proximity where some of the staff will have lived, and there is the first reference to a market, which could well have been in existence since Domesday.

From a decade later there is an even more remarkable account of the manor in the form of a survey made between 1283 and 1285 for Archbishop Pecham (1279-92). This is one of the surveys of the archbishop's seventeen manors across Kent. Each was obviously written by a local man in the way that suited the local organisation best, and Charing is one of the fullest of the seventeen.

This makes clear that most of the manor lay in Charing and Egerton parishes. The demesne, which still seems to have been farmed out, consisted of 155 acres of arable in Westfield and 67½ acres in Eastfield. While the locations are not identified, it is likely that they were what came to be called Westcourt and Eastcourt, areas of virtually the same size, drawn on a 1736 map of the manor for the Wheler family who owned the manor at that time (Fig. 2.1). Westfield/Westcourt lay to the west of the High Street and north of the road from Lenham, i.e. under the present housing estate and covering the race course. Eastfield/Eastcourt lay directly behind the manor house, north of Pett Lane. This was the best arable land in the manor, on the highly fertile lower chalk. There were 84½ acres of meadow, probably south towards the Stour, and 334 acres of woodland, some up on the Downs in Longbeech and Rushmere, but perhaps some in the nine dens belonging to the manor, which lay in the Smarden/Biddenden and Cranbrook area.

There is no mention of pasture, although there were obviously animals – as indicated by those in Kilwardby's accounts and the presence of meadow for hay – and it has been suggested that pasture may have been combined with woodland which could have been interspersed by scrub.

The tenants were still divided into several classes. At the top were the freelanders, those whose lands were free of all but honorific services. There were ten of them, and most of their farm names survive: in Charing were Barnfield, Newland, Pett, Acton, and two at Eversley. Others were attached to estates held of the archbishop in surrounding parishes. Two were in Egerton: Richard Young (site unknown), and Barling's, half a mile south-east of Egerton church; Chilston was probably Chilston manor in Boughton Malherbe, and Boughton could also have been in that parish. Thus the 'manor' as described in this survey went someway beyond the boundary of the later ecclesiastical parish of Charing. Most of the names are known to be sub-manors held from the archbishop by knights, who had to provide a fixed quota for military service when required. It is not clear when these were formed, but they may even go back to Saxon times.

Eversley

The manor of Eversley, a sub-manor of Charing, has now all but disappeared, but it was of considerable importance in the thirteenth century. It was sited on the Downs, in the area of Longbeech Wood, and the site of the manor house and surrounding buildings was still shown in Chapel Wood on the tithe map of 1840. The estate was held by Walter of Eversley in the 1220s, and passed to his son Bartholomew, who was partly brought up as a ward of Thomas de Bendyng of Newland, a common practice at the time. By 1249 Bartholomew had married Agnes, who was nurse to Henry III's daughter Beatrice, and they received a grant and later a state pension and royal livery from the Crown. The couple had two sons, Edmund and John. In Pecham's 1283-5 survey of Charing, there were two free holdings at Eversley, one held by John of Eversley and John, son of Walter of Eversley, and the other by John, son of Bartholomew of Eversley. By 1327 the estate was in the hands of the Peyforer family and eventually passed to the Sondes of Throwley and Sheldwich.

Pett

Pett was a sub-manor of the archbishop, and part of the manor of Little Chart. At the time of Domesday it was held by William son of Hermenfried. By the early thirteenth century the family, whether the same one or not, was called 'of Pett'. By the early fourteenth century Pett was held in conjunction with Newcourt, an estate in the area of the present crematorium. The Newcourt family died out around 1500 and the estate passed to Hugh at Hatche, executor to John Newcourt and possibly his brother in law. By the early sixteenth century it belonged to the at Water family of Royton, and Mary at Water brought it with her when she married Robert Honywood in 1543.

There was a chapel at Pett, for which priests were appointed in the thirteenth century, but it was found to be in great decay in the Visitation of 1511; its ruins still survive. The farm associated with the house had a large aisled barn of late fifteenth or even early sixteenth-century date. This has now been turned into a dwelling (Fig. 2.3).

Fig. 2.3
Interior of the aisled
barn at Pett Place
before conversion
(A T Adams, 1988)

Newlands

In the late twelfth century either the Bendyngs or a previous family at Newlands built a fine stone chapel there which still survives in part. It seems to have had a small chancel and two-bay nave, and a south nave aisle (now demolished). Although greatly altered, high quality scalloped capitals and a north doorway with ring (bobbin) mouldings on the arches and jambs still remain (Fig. 2.4). The chapel had passed to Leeds Priory before Archbishop Warham's appointees conducted a Visitation in 1511-12, when it was noted that neither the chantry nor the chapel were being kept up, and that the case against the prior was currently before the archbishop. The chapel is illustrated on a 1639 map of the Calehill estate, set between the gatehouse and the manor house (Fig. 2.5).

Fig. 2.4 Newlands chapel. The north doorway (S Pearson)

Newlands (Newland in the Middle Ages) was likewise a sub-manor and free holding, located at the southern edge of the parish. It was held by the Bendyng family who are known from the early thirteenth century. They seem to have had good connections in Kent, for Adam de Bendyng, who died in 1229, was married to Alice of Thurnham, whose father Stephen was a royal seneschal (steward), and grandfather a constable of Saltwood Castle. These were not the only thirteenth-century Bendyngs in the county, and it would be unwise to speculate too far on the detail of the family connections. It appears that Newlands passed to the Brockhulls of Calehill, and was sold to John Darell in 1410-11.

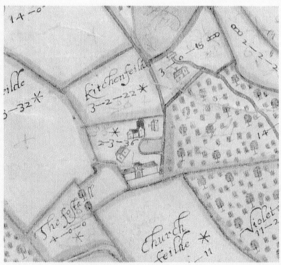

Fig. 2.5 Newlands manor; detail from the 1639 map of the Calehill estate showing the manor house complex and mill site (Centre for Kentish Studies: Map U386/P1; © Kent Archives and Local History Services, Kent County Council)

Burleigh

Burleigh is a farm on the western edge of the parish. Its history is unclear. According to Hasted it belonged to a family of that name, and Sir John de Burleigh founded a chantry [no date] for a priest to sing for his soul and those of his family. It does not appear as one of the free lands in 1283-5, but in 1310 land in Burleigh, formerly said to have been held by John de Barnfield, was held by a Ruxley who was listed in 1283-5 as holding free land at Barnfield, so the two estates may have been held together.

The 1639 map of the Calehill estate shows two sites at Burleigh (Fig. 2.6). To the east, called Burleigh farm, is a large manor house forming an H or U plan, perhaps where the present farmhouse stands, with its associated outbuildings and gardens.

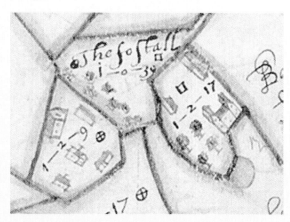

Fig. 2.6 Burleigh manor; detail from the 1639 map of the Calehill estate. The map legend indicates that plots marked with a cross in a circle belonged to Burleigh chantry, while plots marked by a square are simply called Burleigh (Centre for Kentish Studies: Map U386/P1; © Kent Archives and Local History Services, Kent County Council)

On a second plot to the west are illustrated the chantry chapel, two houses and a couple of outhouses. Today the chapel is said to be an overgrown ruin remaining in the middle of a field. A fifteenth-century timber-framed house next to it, which was re-erected in Egerton in the 1960s, was reputedly the priest's house and was certainly one of the two houses depicted on the map.

Below the freelands were gavel lands. These were also freeholds, but the gavelmen also owed money rents and labour services which were organised by the sulung. The rents, at 2d an acre, were the lowest on the manor but the highest in all the archbishop's estates. There was also a render of hens and eggs (12 hens and 160 eggs per sulung), and the tenants had to perform various tasks such as ploughing, reaping and carting. There were thirty-one gavel-land holdings, some held by more than one person, and many people had part of more than one holding. Freelanders could also hold gavel land, since it was not necessary for a man to do his own work for the lord – he simply had to make sure that someone performed the services on his behalf.

In the next level down were twenty-one 'inlands' or 'five acres'. These tenancies had probably once been part of the demesne and were usually subject to tight control. The size was small (hence 'five acres'), and services fairly onerous, including everything required of gavel-land tenants, plus carrying services – for example fetching salt or fish – and tiling or thatching manorial buildings.

There were nineteen woodland or Wealden lands for which the tenants paid money rents and hens and eggs. Some were known as 'dens' and their tenants could have five pigs foraging freely in the woods without paying dues, but they had to provide timber for manorial buildings and work it as required; and if the archbishop needed to fell timber and cart it through their corn, they were not to complain!

Two kinds of holding were probably new and held for money rent only. They may have originated as a result of the pressure for land that occurred as the population increased during the thirteenth century. 121 acres of woodland, probably on the Downs in Longbeech and Rushmere, were divided into twenty-two holdings of varying sizes and rents. Men like Henry Carbonel (i.e. charcoal burner) held several pieces. Then there were fifty-four pieces of 'inland' or 'foreland', probably reclaimed land let for economic rents. In addition there was now a watermill and a windmill. The watermill was probably associated with the water system to the south and east of what is now called Clewards, the green space to the south of the manor house. The site of the windmill is unknown, but 'windmill field' is marked on a 1639 map of the Calehill estate in Burleigh Road opposite what is now the railway station.

The smallest holdings of all were nineteen cotlands, the holders possibly descendants of the slaves of Domesday. The rents were so high (1s 4d an acre) that Kenneth Witney, who published the survey, thought that the services listed had been commuted to money rents. They included weeding, digging, reaping, maintaining buildings, driving pigs to the dens, making hay, folding their animals in the lord's field (so the lord got the benefit of the manure), threshing in return for food and grain, and supplying malt in return for wood. In addition, when the archbishop came to stay, the cotlanders had to provide two men in the kitchen, two in the bake house and two in the brew house. The holdings were between half an acre and three acres, which was less than was required for subsistence, and since several of the men had craft names, such as Nigel the Tanner, Thomas Smith, Henry Carbonel, William at Windmill, John Tailor and Thomas Chapman, it looks as though they did not depend for their livelihoods on farming alone.

The final rents were for market stalls. There appear to have been three markets, though two of them might have been fairs since they were located away from the settlement and paid smaller rents only once or twice a year. Twenty-four stalls were in Westlese, where rents were charged twice a year for a total sum of 6d each. The holders mostly held land in the manor as well. It is not clear where Westlese was. But in 1814 the 'fair field' was part of Westfield/ Westcourt, just north-west of the village, and the 1840 tithe map shows it in the north-east corner of the field, below the Pilgrims' Way, now partly under the A252 and the housing estate. The second market had thirty-five stalls at Ray (Raywood), south of the village. The stall holders paid between ½d and 2d, some once, some twice a year. These holders were not called 'of' like most of the first ones, but were largely 'at' Brook, Windmill, Ray, Gate etc., suggesting they were of fairly lowly status.

The third group of sixteen market rents were higher and varied more in kind and value. This market was clearly in the centre of the settlement near the gates of the manor house. Several rents were specifically for market stalls: Elena the ale-wife paid 1d for a site that had been Walter the Mason's, and William Shoemaker paid 6d on behalf of Alicia the laundress. Other rents may have been for houses in the village. For example, William the Clerk paid the high sum of 3s 4d for a site to the west of the lord's garden, and Henry Carbonel, who also had woodland for his charcoal burning, paid 6d for a wine store in the market, and 2s for an inn. This reference to an inn is unique in the Pecham surveys; none is found in the other manors even though they included towns like Maidstone, Westgate in Canterbury,

Wingham and Wrotham. Most references to inns occur from the late fourteenth century onwards, but they must have originated before then and this is one of the earliest mentioned in documents. The 1736 map of the manorial demesne shows that, unlike most of the village, the area to the west of the manor precinct, on the east side of the High Street, belonged to the estate (Fig. 2.2). This is where The Swan Inn (now Elizabethan Court) was later located, and it could already have been the site of the inn mentioned in the survey. The Market Place was labelled to the south of the manor house.

This was Charing at the high point of the Middle Ages. Although no houses survive from this period, it can be inferred from the third set of market rents and the names of some of the 'five acre' tenants and cotlanders that a sizeable proportion of the population lived in a nucleated settlement or village near the manor house, in the area where Charing Town as we know it developed. In contrast, the dwellings of the majority of those who farmed larger holdings were almost certainly scattered throughout the manor. Many of the farm names are those still in use today, and the names of some tenants, for example 'at Ray' or 'of Greenhill' (in Egerton), also make this clear. Dispersed settlements of this kind were everywhere in Kent.

The Black Death and afterwards

During the thirteenth century both population and prices increased but for many people the standard of living declined, and in the early fourteenth century the situation in a manor such as Charing changed dramatically. A long succession of rural problems, including failed harvests and cattle disease, led to periods of famine. This was exacerbated by the king requiring higher taxes to support the Hundred Years War, and the commandeering of supplies to feed the army meant less produce being available for local consumption. We have no records of what occurred in Charing, but it cannot have been an easy time for the tenants. Then, if the Black Death of 1348-9 hit Charing as hard as elsewhere, between a third and a half of the population was killed off. This was followed by droughts and further epidemics in the 1360s and 1370s.

We do not know how many inhabitants there were before the plague struck, but in 1377 we learn that 221 people over the age of fourteen paid the poll tax in Charing. If the catchment area was the same as at Domesday (a very big 'if'), and accounting for children below the age of fourteen, there might have been a total of around 300, which was not more and may have been fewer than estimated at Domesday. However, the survivors of the fourteenth-century catastrophes tended to prosper. They were able to demand higher wages, there was more food to go round, and those who had land were often able to buy the holdings of families that had gone under. The period c.1380-c.1420 is when the first substantial timber-framed farmhouses that still survive in Charing were built. More remain from the fifteenth century and household goods indicate a high standard of living, at least among the better-off. Charing men were perhaps less dissatisfied with their lot than elsewhere, for no one is known to have joined the national uprising of 1381, or the Kentish rebellion of Jack Cade in 1450, which took place at a time of severe recession.

In 1398 a short survey of the manor after the death of Archbishop Arundel shows a rather different picture from 100 years earlier. The amount of arable land in demesne was significantly reduced, whether for shortage of labour or less demand for produce. Instead, there was pasture for livestock: sheep in 75½ acres of Westfield and large animals in various woods on and below the Downs. Although there was a serjeant of the manor with responsibility for husbandry, one John Best appears to have been farming the demesne lands for a rent of £20 a year. After the Black Death the demesnes, which had for a century or more been farmed directly by the archbishop's staff, were once again leased – a practice which was judged to be economically more efficient in a time when returns were low – and this remained the case until the Reformation. Among the assets mentioned for the first time in this short survey was a tile house valued at 26s 8d, complete with clay, lime and wood required for burning tiles.

By this time there are many documents associated with the archbishops and the manor of Charing. Registers indicate when the archbishops came to stay and record grants of land and appointments to positions; accounts provide evidence of manorial expenditure. In addition, extant wills of the period shed light on how the better-off lived.

We can see that Charing was not an isolated place in the later Middle Ages. Not only was there traffic into the village through the comings and goings of the archbishop and his staff, or the manor's relations with other archiepiscopal manors across Kent, but the inhabitants themselves had connections beyond the parish boundaries. Humphrey Barrey, for example, who died in 1431, asked to be buried at Senyton [Sevington] church near Ashford and left bequests to the churches of Charing, Sevington, Ashford, Warehorne and Horton Priory, as well as to St Augustine's Abbey and two friaries in Canterbury. Thomas Paunsherst, senior, who died in 1472 not only left the manor of Broughton [sic] to one son, but a tenement and a windmill in Sandwich to another. Simon Pepyr (d.1483) drew the trustees of his estate from Charing, Pluckley, Stalisfield and Throwley, while his wife, who died a year later, had lands in Storringden, Monkton, Wichling and Doddington. Although these must have been among the wealthier inhabitants, they show that despite bad roads and the slow speed of travel people could have personal connections across most of central and east Kent.

The wills also provide insight into the standards of living of the better-off during the fifteenth century. Humphrey Barrey had six silver cups which were divided among his children. Florence Halden, who came from Boardfield on the Downs and was married successively to William at Gate and John Halden, had twelve silver spoons and four silk belts to bequeath in 1470. Julia Rotinge, who died in 1497, had three pairs of linen sheets and a table cloth, bed hangings and items of brass and pewter to leave. Linen counted among people's most valued possessions. When William Brent of Peirce House died in 1496 his probate inventory, one of the earliest in Kent, valued his linen at £11 2s 8d, which was more than the combined value of the goods in any single room of his house.

Farming was obviously the major occupation of people wealthy enough to leave wills. In Kent, unlike most of the rest of England, inheritance was not governed by primogeniture. Instead it was ruled by the laws of gavelkind, a pre-Conquest system under which property could be bought or sold at will, but when a person died his inheritance had to be divided equally between his sons, or daughters if there were no sons. The ability to dispose of land freely and the obligation to divide the inheritance led to an active land market among tenant farmers, and if a man could afford to do so, he built up separate holdings for each son and bequeathed named tenements and fields to each one. The result was an endless accumulation and division of estates.

Widows also had to be provided for. Some men, particularly those who died young, left everything to their wives and dictated complex arrangements for the children's eventual

The Brent family of Peirce House

The Brent family seem to have arrived in Charing from Somerset in the middle of the fifteenth century. They were already of gentry status, and did not take long to establish themselves as a major Charing family, running one of the only known farms located in the village centre. They lived at Peirce House (Fig. 2.7), although it is probable that the open hall, the earliest part of the dwelling to survive, was built before their time. Hugh Brent is recorded as buying lands in Charing as well as Little Chart, Stalisfield, Pluckley, Smarden and Lynsted from the 1430s onwards. His name is mentioned as the 'farmer' of the Charing manor demesne from the 1450s, although other farmers are also listed in the 1460s. Nonetheless, this seems to have become something of a hereditary tenure as several leases to later Brents survive in the early sixteenth century. Wills and inventories, discussed elsewhere in this book, show how important the family became in the development of the parish church and the building of Peirce House.

Fig. 2.7 Peirce House, High Street (S Dray)

inheritance. But when the children were adult they often received most of the inheritance directly, and husbands sometimes specified exactly what their widows were entitled to. Ruffus Clerk in 1476 left his tenement and land to his son, but his wife was to have two chambers at the west end of the house, one upstairs, one down. Richard Walyngeham's wife was to have the north end of his house, access to fire, water and fuel, as well as a cow and a hog. Thomas Foxton willed that his wife should have five acres of land, an allowance from his son, a chamber and access to the fire etc, plus a cow and as much land as required to grow a 'tolfet' of hemp. For a woman who had been mistress in her own home the change to widowhood might be dramatic unless she was on good terms with her offspring. If she was young enough she usually married again.

Little can be learnt about occupations other than farming from this handful of early wills, although there are clues. Thomas Ovyngton, who died in 1460, left his wife all his estate for the term of her life. After her death one son was to have all the lands north of the highway, while his second son, William, was to have the tile house and twenty acres on the south side of the highway. If this was the road from Lenham, it could be describing Tile Lodge Farm, which might have been the archbishop's tile house mentioned above. Lawrence Broke left seventeen cartloads of stone for repairing roads around Charing, an amount that suggests rather more than the picking up of flints on downland fields, and perhaps indicates a man engaged in quarrying. Julia Rotinge left twelve cider casks among her other goods, suggesting she was involved in cider making on a commercial scale.

Fragmentary information among the papers of the Darells of Calehill informs us of a completely different aspect of life: serving in the army in the early fifteenth century. John Darell was a commissioner of array, i.e. charged with recruitment, and there is a list of his tenants who were to serve in the army, possibly related to those called up before the Battle of Agincourt. These included five men from Field borough (on the edge of Egerton parish), and six from Sanpett borough, a little further to the east. Each group had one fully armed man with a shield – the man from Sanpett, Johannes Swon, perhaps coming from Swan Street – and five archers. In addition, Henry Colbach of Sanpett borough was armed but appears to have had no shield.

Occasionally, evidence from the manorial papers may also help us to piece together a bit more about the village itself. For example, in the archbishop's accounts for 1442 John Pevington, tiler, was paid for 9,500 tiles and tiling the manor house helped by a servant; in 1458 Thomas Pevington and a servant were likewise paid for tiling. Tiling was a constant requirement at the manor house, although these are the only occasions when the tilers are named. Whether they were associated with the archbishop's tile house is unknown. Wills of 1464 and 1484 survive for John and Thomas Pevington respectively, and they were probably father and son. Neither mentions tiling; their wills were only concerned with the distribution of messuages (dwellings and their curtilages) and 'pieces' of land, which sound like small holdings. This is what might be expected of craftsmen who farmed small plots of land, perhaps five acres or less, in addition to practising their trade.

During the middle of the fifteenth century there was another period of distress and recession, but by the late fifteenth century rural life had become easier again and many men of 'yeomen' status, in other words the gavelkinders, were simply farming or combining farming with profitable occupations, and were enjoying a period of prosperity which lasted into the early sixteenth century. These are the people who emerge from the documents. At this date there is little information about the labouring poor beneath them.

Chapter 3: Early Modern Charing

by Sarah Pearson and Pat Winzar

Religion and the Reformation

In early Tudor times the people of Charing must have been familiar with the sight of their king – a privilege not granted to most of the king's subjects. Henry VII was a guest of the archbishop eight times between 1498 and 1508. Henry VIII came twice in 1511 and stayed for nearly two weeks in 1513. There was then a gap, but he came again in June 1520 with Queen Catherine of Aragon and a massive entourage, on his way to meet the king of France, Francis I, for a spectacular state occasion known as the 'Field of Cloth of Gold', which was held near Calais. Finally, he made three further visits between 1541 and 1544. Judging by the account of entertaining the abbot of Faversham 200 years earlier (see p.91) many local people must have been employed in preparations for these visits, however menial their roles, and all the inhabitants would have had a chance to see the royal visitor at some point. Little did they know that in 1545 the king would force Archbishop Cranmer to give him the manor of Charing in return for a much less attractive property in east Kent so that it became known henceforth as the 'Royal Manor of Charing'. But by then Henry was not a well man and he died in 1547 without coming again. Under Queen Mary the manor was briefly returned to Cardinal Pole, who became archbishop of Canterbury in 1556. But since both he and the queen died in 1558 this hardly broke the royal tenure. As far as we know, no royal lord of the manor ever visited Charing again.

By the 1540s the atmosphere surrounding these visits must have changed as the Reformation gathered pace. Archbishop Warham (1503-1532), who was lord of the manor in the early sixteenth century, was a powerful figure both in Kent and at court. He had been in favour of reforming the church in England, but was not in favour of a split with Rome and nor was he a Protestant. However, he died before the issue came to a head and his successor, Archbishop Cranmer, was far more sympathetic to Protestants and more compliant to the king's demands. In 1533 Henry divorced Catherine of Aragon, the main reason for the split with Rome, and married Anne Boleyn. In 1534 the Act of Supremacy was passed, making Henry head of the Church of England. All male subjects had to swear allegiance and priests were ordered to remove all reference to the pope and preach the supremacy. In 1536 the suppression of the monasteries began. Although Charing was not directly affected by the Dissolution, the news must have reverberated, particularly in a county which contained some of the wealthiest monasteries in England, and with monastic estates nearby at Westwell and Lenham. By the time the king came to Charing in 1541 a great deal had taken place since his last visit.

We know little about the effect of the Reformation on Charing and its inhabitants. By the mid 1530s there was a core of priests in Kent with firm Protestant beliefs – among them Henry Godrick of nearby Hothfield – but many parish priests were still very traditional. In Charing, the familiarity of priest and parishioners with the archbishop and the likelihood of a royal visit probably predisposed them to accept the Act of Supremacy without demur, so the parish was unlikely to have been fruitful ground for either radical or ultra-conservative

---

The Brent and Dering families of Peirce House and Wickens

The Brent family of Peirce House remained important to Charing until the middle of the sixteenth century. In the early sixteenth century they enlarged and rebuilt Peirce House (Fig. 7.13, Map 2.36), and, as well as running their own farm, leased the farm of Charing manor in 1528 and 1541. Another Brent owned Wickens, on the eastern edge of the parish. Unfortunately, the two relevant sons of John Brent, who died in 1565, themselves died shortly after and both properties passed to a daughter, Margaret, who was married to John Dering of Surrenden Dering in Pluckley. Two of Margaret and John's younger sons, Anthony and Christopher, inherited Peirce House and Wickens respectively. Anthony does not seem to have prospered; both he and his eldest son, Finch, had numerous children who all had to be provided for. Finch's eldest son, Brent, married the daughter of the vicar; he sold much of his land and probably the house to Gabriel Peirce, and seems to have had little to leave his widow when he died in 1645 for in the 1650s and 1660s the churchwardens' accounts show that funds were provided to repair her house. Where she lived is uncertain, for in 1664 Mr Gabriel Peirce paid the hearth tax on eight hearths in Charing Town (almost certainly Peirce House), while Widow Dering had a single hearth exempt from payment. She died in 1666.

The Derings of Wickens were better-off than the Peirce House branch of the family, and Christopher probably built the decorative timber-framed house we see today (Fig. 7.15). The house remained with his descendants, some of whom lived there, although Anthony Aucher, gent., paid tax there on six hearths in 1664.

---

views. Churches had to purchase the Bible in English and were supposed to remove images and provide registers for births, marriages and deaths, but neither Henry nor the majority of priests were wholeheartedly in favour of dispensing with Catholicism. Not until Edward VI came to the throne in 1547 was Protestantism pursued with vigour. The Latin Mass was abolished; English was compulsory for all services; and priests were no longer required to be celibate. A little further south, Pluckley and Smarden obtained new Protestant incumbents, and in that area there were stirrings of even more radical dissent. But Charing seems never to have been affected this way and its priests largely followed the edicts of the day: first those of the Protestant reform, then the reversal to Catholicism when Mary became queen in 1553 (although it has been suggested that a married priest may have been forcibly removed at that time), and finally the change back to Protestant worship under Queen Elizabeth in 1558. However bewildering these rapid changes were, the monarch was lord of the manor of Charing and loyalty to their lord was probably natural to most people.

As far as we know, the only committed and outspoken Protestants in the parish were the Honywoods of Pett. Mary, the daughter of Robert at Water of Royton in Lenham, took Pett in marriage to Robert Honywood in 1543. She is recorded by contemporary writers as having supported Protestant martyrs under Queen Mary, writing to them, visiting them in prison, and attending the burning of one John Bradford in 1555. She was in contact with both John Foxe, who wrote *The Book of Martyrs*, published in 1563, and with the puritan preacher, Edward Dering, a relative of the Derings of Surrenden Dering in Pluckley. There were few other gentry of importance in the parish. The next nearest were the Darells of Calehill in Little Chart, who held much of the land in the southern part of the parish from the manor of Charing. They were certainly traditionalists, and probably had problems with the Protestant ascendancy when it was prevalent. After the Restoration of the monarchy in 1660 they became recusant Catholics.

In 1676 a national tally of religious belief was made called the Compton Census. Parish priests were ordered to list the number of communicants (i.e. those over the age of sixteen) and also any Catholics and dissenters. Charing had 291 conformists, no papists, and thirteen non-conformists. At this time there was no dissenters' chapel in the parish, but in 1672 Daniel Kingsnorth had been licensed to preach at Baptist meetings held in the house of Thomas Hill. There is a further certificate for meetings (denomination not stated) in the home of Robert Wilson in 1715, and the Methodist chapel was built on land purchased in 1814.

Politics, war and the gentry

Religious beliefs had a direct effect on the political allegiances of the gentry. This became painfully apparent during the seventeenth century as concerns grew over the Stuart monarchy's lavish expenditure, excessive taxation, and promotion of increasingly Anglo-Catholic religion and its own role as head of the church. Although conservatives in religion tended to be royalist, and were certainly not Republicans, many of them were disturbed by these tendencies. On the other hand ardent Protestants, increasingly puritan in outlook, were anti-royalist and came to support Parliament and Commonwealth. As occurred across Kent, the land-owning gentry in and around Charing were split in their views.

Charing itself had no major players in county politics of the period, probably because the fact that the manor was first archiepiscopal and then royal meant that few prominent gentry families emerged in the parish. Sir Edward Dering of Pluckley (1598-1644), was an important county figure during the difficult time before the Civil War, and the Darells of Calehill were closely associated with him. He was a complex man who disliked extremism on either side. He hoped that moderate religious reform could unite the country, and as a member of the Long Parliament in 1640 he was in opposition to Charles I. But as moderating views were rejected and the situation deteriorated, he became an active royalist and joined the king's side. He defected, however, when Parliament offered an amnesty to royalists in 1643, possibly because he was already extremely ill, returning to Surrenden to die in 1644. In 1643 his estates and those of Sir Robert Darell were sequestered, although they were both later regained. Not unnaturally lesser branches of the Derings, by then established at Peirce House and Wickens in Charing, supported Sir Edward. After Sir Edward's death, the Derings and Darells formed part of the Kentish opposition to the Commonwealth, and the next Sir Edward Dering was returned to the first Restoration parliament in 1660 as one of the two knights of the shire. Nicholas Gilborne, later Sir Nicholas, who apparently came from London and was the lessee of Charing manor house and demesne farm in the years to either side of 1600, was a Justice of the Peace in 1596 and became High Sherriff of Kent in 1611. His descendants were royalists and his grandson and family had to go into exile on the continent during the Commonwealth.

The Honywoods of Pett, mentioned earlier, were committed Protestants and, as might be expected, they sympathised with the Parliamentarians during the Civil War. However, Sir Robert Honywood the elder, the grandson of the first Robert, was a moderate, and although a member of the County Committee for Parliament in 1643, he defected. His

Digital image copyright of Kent County Council

Fig. 3.1 Map of the Calehill estate, 1639 with amendments 1678. Lands in Charing parish are largely to the north and west (top and left of the map). The southern part of the estate was in Egerton and Little Chart parishes. (Centre for Kentish Studies: Map U386/P1; © Kent Archives and Local History Services, Kent County Council)

son, the younger Sir Robert, was a member of the Kent County Committee for the Rump Parliament in 1659-1660 and was known to associate with committed Republicans. His main claim to fame, however, lay as a diplomat in Europe during the Commonwealth, when he helped negotiate a peace between the kings of Sweden and Denmark. Although he was not pursued after the Restoration, his political career may have terminated (he was already fifty-nine in 1660) as he turned to translating a history of Venice. In 1667 his eldest son, also Robert, was attainted for treason after serving with the Dutch against the English in the second Anglo-Dutch war, and when the father published his translation from Italian in 1673 he wrote that he had turned to this task in an uncomfortable old age and ruined fortune, brought upon him by public calamity.

From the Middle Ages until after the Civil War, all men between the ages of sixteen and sixty had to join the militia, with the gentry being responsible for making sure they were properly trained and ready to be called up at any time. In 1608 Robert Darell of Calehill was commissioned captain of the military band for the hundred of Calehill, as his father John had been before him, and in 1644 Brent Dering of Charing also served as a captain. Among the Calehill papers is a 1608 list of men and arms for the upper hundred of Calehill (in which Charing lay). There were nine corslets (body armour for pike men), nine calivers (small, light muskets) and four muskets; possibly these numbers refer only to the boroughs of Field and Sanpett in the south of the parish where the Darell estates were located. Armour was sometimes listed in probate inventories. Finch Dering, gentlemen, had one armour and a pick axe in 1625, while Ralph Bartlett, glover, owned a musket in 1629. We have no information as to whether the men of Charing ever saw action, either at home or abroad.

Farming the land

The mixed farming practised in Charing in the Middle Ages, continued throughout this period. Apart from the manorial demesne with its huge fields on the Lower Chalk, it was a region of hamlets of two or three dwellings or isolated farmhouses working small farms, many of which were only a few acres in extent. On the Downs to the north poor quality arable land was mixed with the woodland which also covered the scarp. The chalk and gault clay of the shallow valley where the village and demesne were located were good for arable and sheep. Further south, on the Lower Greensand, small fields enclosed by hedges or shaws (strips of woodland) were largely pastoral but there were also experiments with hops, flax and fruit. Other parts of the sandstone were heathlands occupied by commons.

Farm size and field layout are indicated on a 1639 map of the Calehill estate, amended in 1678 (Fig. 3.1). At that time the manor of Newlands had thirty-two parcels of land containing just over 301 acres; Burleigh farm occupied 180 acres; and Burleigh chantry lands, in nineteen parcels, came to just over 130 acres. But many holdings were much smaller. Thomas Cooke at Hunger Hatch had twenty-three acres in five parcels, and in 1678 Anthony Baldock of Little Swan Street Farm, had only one parcel of just over one acre. However, in 1629 Richard Baldock, possibly Anthony's father, held land from the manor of Charing, so the Baldocks and others with very small acreages on the Calehill map are likely to have been farming fields belonging to other landowners whose names are summarily indicated beside the detailed information on the map. The sites of the various farms mentioned are shown on Map 1.

The common heath at Brockton is illustrated on the 1639 map. It remained open as Charing heath until the nineteenth century, and part is still common, used as playing fields. Calehill heath was an early hunting park and warren for rabbits. It had been part of a small manor called Stilley, and became the property of the Darells. It was only partly in Charing parish, including the road junction known as the 'Pin Cushion', now underneath the High Speed Rail Link, where gallows are sometimes said to have been located. When enclosed in the nineteenth century part remained open as the recreation ground of Westwell Leacon. A further common, at Raywood, was enclosed in the early seventeenth century. When ninety acres of heath belonging to Charing manor were leased from the Crown by one Edward Bee Esq. of Essex, he discovered that the common rights of the adjoining tenants meant it was little use to him; so when he bought the land in 1622 he agreed to partition it, retaining half for his sole use, with the rest divided among the neighbouring tenants. Some of the divisions can be seen on the 1639 map.

Wills and probate inventories indicate how important farming was. At the upper end of the scale a man such as Matthew Fryday, yeoman, whose goods were valued at £255 7s when he died in June 1660, had a sizeable house (nine rooms), six acres of wheat and thirteen of barley, oats, peas, tares (vetch) and hemp in the ground, and twelve acres of meadow. He owned four cows, two calves, two oxen, two horses, three hogs and a sow. In addition he had wheat, barley, oats, hay and peas in the barn, and 110lbs of cheese in store. But many poorer men also farmed in a small way. Abraham Best, linen weaver, who died in April 1624 with goods valued at £15 9s, not only had hemp for his loom, but had sown one and a half acres each of wheat and peas, had wheat, barley and malt in store, and owned a pig. Thomas Austen, husbandman, who died in December 1675 worth only £9 12s, had wheat in the ground (amount unspecified), oats and hemp in store, a cow (this was his most valuable possession, assessed at £3 10s), six sheep and a pig. Except for some who were traders, most parishioners wealthy enough to leave wills had farming interests.

Personal details relating to farming are few and far between. Thomas Adman, yeoman, died in March 1569. This was in the middle of a period of rapid inflation, so his inventory, valued at £20 6s 10d, was the equivalent of a £40 inventory a hundred years later. Apart from various crops in store, five cows and twenty-eight sheep of varying age, he left his son the south end of the barn in which to store ladders, trestles and other equipment to be used twice a year at Charing fair, and his wife the apples from four named trees: a pownwalter, a white mylche, an old wiffe and a rysminde. Others had fruit trees, or apples in store, but this is the only time the varieties of apple were named.

Gavelkind or partible inheritance, the partitioning of property equally between sons, was still in force in seventeenth-century Kent, and Charing has an unusually clear example of the results at Barnfield, a farm on the southern edge of the parish. The house is a large medieval hall house, originally consisting of a central open hall flanked by two, two-storied ends with a parlour and chamber above to the north, and a cross passage, two service rooms and chamber above, to the south. In the sixteenth century a first-floor chamber was inserted over the hall and later the timber frame was hidden by brick and tile-hanging (Fig. 3.2). In 1632 Robert Rayner of Barnfield died and left his son John the north end of the house with seven rooms (including what was probably a detached kitchen), together with the stable, half the barn, his share of the close, an old orchard and a hemp plot. His son Stephen was to have the rest of the house, barn and land. Stephen died in 1633 leaving his share to his sister, who in turn

Fig. 3.2 Barnfield from the south west (S Pearson)

left it to her son, another Stephen. In 1639 the second Stephen left all his lands to a relative, George Rayner of Egerton. Meanwhile, when John died in 1668 his half of the house and lands went to his son, a second Robert. How and when the two halves came back together again is unclear. In 1754 a William Rayner died with what appears to be a whole house in Charing, although we cannot be certain that this was Barnfield. Splitting property did not seem to lead to minute and uneconomical plots of land, which suggests that when the split became too small, one beneficiary sold his inheritance to another. If so, in this case it is possible that George of Egerton sold his half to the second Robert, thereby bringing the property together again. Nonetheless, gavelkind was one factor in keeping farms small.

By the eighteenth century fruit farming and hop growing had become commercially important on the Greensand Ridge further west where Sir Edward Filmer of East Sutton was experimenting with new crops. In Charing, a lack of eighteenth-century probate inventories makes it difficult to gauge the extent to which changes in farming practice were taking place. But when the inventory of George Sayer of Pett was taken in June 1718, he had a large quantity of hops in the granary, and a 1752 map of the Pett estate marks several fields both in the Vale of Holmesdale and up on the Downs as hop fields. The map illustrates the sizeable house, outbuildings and large farm, together with extensive gardens and orchards (Fig. 3.3).

Roads

In the seventeenth century the coach road from Maidstone to Ashford is said to have passed through the southern part of the parish. The 1639 Calehill map shows it coming from Lenham Heath, to the north of Charing heath, turning right and then left, passing south of Newlands and then eastwards across Calehill heath, where it was named the road from London to Ashford; at this point there was a north turn to Charing along what is now the Pluckley Road. A second road from Maidstone lay on the line of the A20 west of Charing. It was called the Shire Way on the 1639 Calehill estate map and turned left at the High Street, right along Pett Lane to the north of the manor house, and continued past Pett into Westwell parish; it is clearer on the 1736 map of the Wheler estate (Fig.2.1), where it is labelled 'Lenham road' to the west and 'Ashford road' to the east of the village. Neither of these routes was particularly quick or convenient, so it must have been a relief when the turnpike was made in 1785. This meant that traffic from Lenham to Charing village came in along School Road, turned south instead of north, and continued along the newly created Old Ashford Road and nearby section of what is now the A20; it was a much easier route than the previous one along Pett Lane.

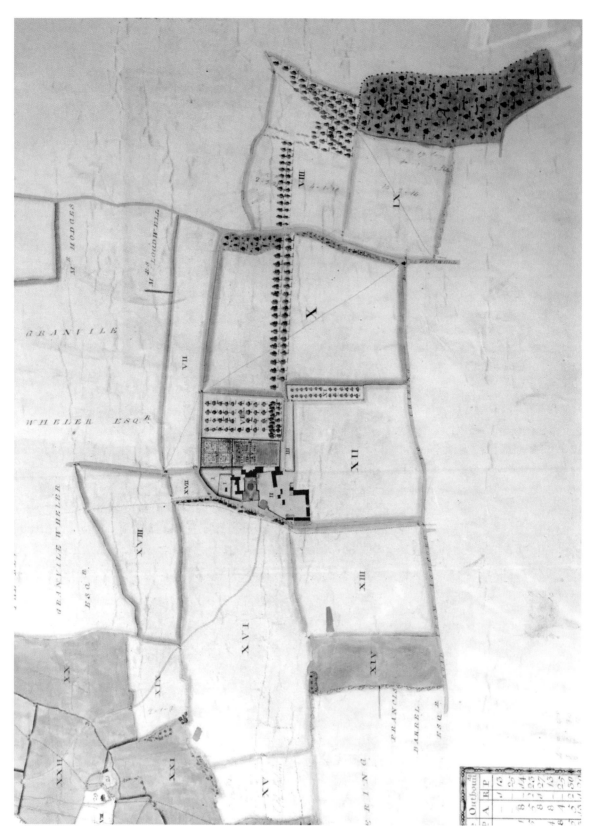

Fig. 3.3 Part of a map of the Pett estate, 1752. North is to the top, so Charing village is off the map to the left and the avenue of trees runs northwards from the house to the Pilgrims' Way and beyond. (Private collection)

Trade and Occupations

Well before 1500 timber-framed houses which incorporated purpose-built shops had been built in the High Street, indicating that trading had largely moved from the market to permanent shops during the fourteenth and fifteenth centuries. This led to the decline of the market itself. In addition, there was the twice yearly fair, which still took place outside Charing, probably in the great west field just to the north of the village, now partly under the A252 and partly on the racecourse. This is where 'Fair Field' was marked on the 1840 tithe map. In the seventeenth century the fair was known as a place to buy Welsh cattle, which may be part of the reason for Charing's thriving leather trade at that time.

The number of households in Charing parish in the seventeenth century can only be estimated from the number of householders recorded for the national hearth tax of 1664. The tax was collected by borough, not parish, and the two seldom coincided. Charing was covered by five boroughs: Charing Town, Acton to the west (which possibly ran into Lenham), Highslade to the east (which may have included part of Westwell) and Sanpett and Field to the south (which may respectively have run into Little Chart and Egerton parishes). 170 names were listed, of whom forty-eight were exempted, and there were probably other poor families whose names escaped the lists altogether. Calculating population at this period can only be approximate, but if 170 households had an average of 4.5 residents (a generally recognised figure), there may have been around 765 people in the five boroughs. In 1676 the Compton Census records 304 communicants and non-dissenters in Charing parish which, allowing for those under sixteen who did not yet take communion, possibly means around 500 people of all ages living in the parish itself.

In Charing Town a manorial rental dated 1646 listed some thirty houses. In the hearth tax of 1664 thirty-two householders in the Town were charged and twenty-four were exempted, indicating a total of fifty-six households. As discussed in Chapter 7, at least twenty-five of the dwellings that still survive in the village date to the seventeenth century or earlier. Since these documents were concerned with households rather than houses, the surviving buildings were probably home to more than twenty-five families. Written records such as rentals, church registers, churchwardens' accounts, quarter sessions records, court rolls and maps, together with wills and probate inventories, have all been used to compile the list of seventeenth-century occupations in Table 3.1. This is not a statistical analysis but aims to illustrate the pattern of trading over the course of the century. In addition to the retailers, all trades essential for the support of a town in a rural area were there: smiths, woodworkers, limeburners, colliers or charcoal burners, and the ropemakers who supplied hemp ropes for wells and church bells.

The following sections provide further details of the trades and those who practised them. To help make sense of the currency quoted it is worth noting that £1 in 1600 money would, depending on the source used, be worth around £200–£225 today (2011) and £1 in 1700 money would be worth around £135–£165.

The leather industry

The leather industry was important in Charing. Butchers, tanners, fellmongers (dealers in hide or skins), shoemakers, cordwainers (high class shoemakers) and glovers made an economic chain. There ought to have been a saddler, but one is not named. One of the fellmongers was Thomas Killam who died in 1674. His inventory, valued at £70, included

Table 3.1: Trading patterns in Charing during the seventeenth century

Trade	1590-1610	1611-1620	1621-1630	1631-1640	1641-1650	1651-1660	1661-1670	1671-1680	1681-1690	1691-1700
Cloth										
Clothier	3	1	2	2	1					
Kerseymaker	1	2	3	2						
Linen weaver	2		1	1	1	1			1	
Tailor	2	4	1	1		1				
Fuller		1								
Hempdresser	2	2	1							
Ropemaker	3	1								
Leather										
Tanner		1	1	2	1	1		1	1	1
Fellmonger					2	2	2	1	1	
Glover	1	1	2							
Cordwainer									1	
Shoemaker	3	2	1							
Metal										
Blacksmith	1	1	2	2	1	1	1			
Whitesmith	1	1								
Metalworker	2	1	1							
Tinker	1									
Armourer				1						
Wood										
Carpenter	3	3	2	1	1	1				
Joiner	1	1	3	1						
Sawyer	1		1							
Trugger	1	1								
Wheelwright		1	1	1						
Food & Drink										
Grocer	1	1	1	1	1	2	1	1		
Miller	1	1	2	3	2	2	2	1		
Alehousekeeper	2									
Innkeeper	1		1		1					1
Butcher	3	3	2	1	2	2	1	1	1	
Rippier		1	1	1						
Maltster		2	1	1						
Miscellaneous										
Physician/surgeon		1								
Chirurgeon		1	1	1			1	1	1	1
Teacher	2			1						
Midwife				2						
Tilemaker		1	1	1	1	1	1			
Tiler	1		1							
Brickmaker				1			1			
Bricklayer				1						
Limeburner	2			1			1			
Collier	1					1	1	1		
Thatcher	2									
Gardener			1					1		

The table is based on information from a variety of sources, but since the documents are not comprehensive, it cannot be taken as a complete record of the Charing trades and occupations practised in each decade. The following principles to measure activity were applied in compilation:

1. Where baptism date only is known, a working life of 30 years from age 20
2. Where burial date only is known, a working life of 30 years backwards from date of death
3. Where baptism and burial are known, working life judged to begin at age 20
4. Where marriage date only known, the decade of that date
5. Where a single other reference is the only source, the decade of the date of that source

wool, skins and pelts, indicating that he was still working at his death. He almost certainly lived at 30 High Street, a small house built *c.*1500 (Fig. 7.7, Map 2.13). Richard Beeching was another fellmonger aged seventy-six when he died in 1690. As a retired man he may have lived with relatives and his inventory wealth totalled only £26. The surviving inventories of two wealthy working Charing fellmongers, for 1711 and 1750, who had large stocks of wool in store and skins at the tanning pits, show that the trade remained important during the eighteenth century.

In the late nineteenth century it was reported that Tanners House, Old Ashford Road (Fig 3.11, Map 2.18), was 'formerly an old tannery and fellmongers place'. Only two of the seventeenth-century tanners left wills: one lived at Barnfield in the Charing Heath area; the whereabouts of the other's dwelling is unknown. The latter's name was Thomas Mitchell and he died in 1698. He was a wealthy man with an inventory valued at £133 16s and property in both Charing and Faversham, where there was also known to be a leather trade.

Two of the glovers died in 1629. One had little except debts owed to him, including £1 by Mr Thomas Dering, a sign that the local gentry patronised Charing traders. The other, Ralph Bartlett, was more prosperous. He left 190 pairs of gloves, each worth between 3d and 4d, indicating that Dering's debt to the first glover was a large one. Bartlett was clearly taken ill while still working, for he had skins to be worked, including sheep, calf and dog, as well as horse and colt hides which he used for making purses. His inventory was valued at £87 6s 4d, and included packs of wool and dressed and undressed leather and hides that were still soaking in lime.

Shoemakers were often relatively poor men, and this was true of Nicholas Younge when he died in 1618. He was only twenty-eight and had few possessions, although there were some pieces of leather and two pairs of shoes in his shop. In contrast, the cordwainer, Thomas Davies, who died in 1693 lived in comfort. He was not working at the time, but with £200 owing to him he may have been receiving an income from money lending, which was a common practice in the days before banks.

The cloth industry

By the later seventeenth century the Kentish cloth industry was declining. Charing lay on the fringe of the woollen cloth weaving area, and its clothiers and kerseymakers (kerseys were lighter woollen cloths than the traditional broadcloths) had ceased to operate by the middle of the century. The kerseymakers seem to have been outworkers, working for clothiers, and only one had woollen yarn and coarse wool waiting to be worked when he died. An inventory survives for one of the clothiers, Joseph Hart, who died in 1644. Totalling £318 3s 1d, it was the most valuable of the seventeenth-century Charing inventories. He only had a small piece of kersey in the house and no looms or wool, but his shop contained twelve pairs of shears, various weights and pressing forms, and there were ninety-five quarters of flax in the house. This suggests that he was mostly engaged in the linen trade, supplying raw material to linen weavers and then finishing the cloth himself.

Linen weaving was clearly important in Charing, with the trade practised in most decades of the century. The linen weavers not only had looms but were husbandmen with small plots of land on which they grew hemp as well as crops. The hemp was used for coarse linen and also ropemaking, so they may have been among those who supplied the hempdressers and ropemakers who were active in the early part of the century.

Metalwork trades

Less is known about the various smiths. Although Simon Beeching, who died in 1670, had a blacksmith's forge with tools and implements in it, there was no mention of iron or of completed items. John Whoper, a whitesmith (tinsmith and finisher of metal goods) who died in 1619 had all the tools and equipment to make pewter and brass vessels, but no raw materials or finished goods. William Killam was called an 'armourer' when he died in 1639, perhaps supplying some of the equipment for the local militia, but neither his will nor his inventory contain information about his craft.

Woodworkers

The wood workers of Charing left no wills or inventories, but something is known about the operations of several carpenters and joiners from payments for work they did refurbishing Charing church after the fire of 1590 (see pp. 67-70). As Chris Currie, who researched the surviving church furniture of the period discovered, much of the furniture was made by local men. Although a pulpit had been made in 1598, a local carpenter, William Amiss, was paid to alter it in 1630, and replace it in 1637. As a carpenter, Amiss was probably not a rich man, something confirmed by the fact that he only paid 6d to a local cess (tax) in 1631, a sum that put him very much at the bottom of the middle rank of taxpayers. Later, he worked at the vicarage, and in the 1660s he repaired the church gate (which had been made by another carpenter, Edward Do, in 1634, who also repaired it on several occasions) and made a frame for the King's Arms in the church. In 1664 the hearth tax return shows him living in a house with only one hearth; he was, however, better off than the twenty-eight per cent of householders who were exempted from paying the tax at all. Other local men, Angell Knowlden and Nicholas Baldock, supplied boards for the church, and Stephen Large, a trugger by trade, was also paid for boards, as well as for smaller wooden items such as shovels and spades.

Food and drink

Retail outlets supplied locals and probably brought people to town. Gentry custom was no doubt important to the traders. For example, the son of Anthony Dering of Peirce House lost a blue coat worth 10s when a local tailor was burgled in 1598. The probate inventory of Richard Dubble, who died while still in business in 1615, shows him to have been trading in woollen and linen cloth, silk, sugar and spices, tobacco and a wide selection of other items. His goods totalled £140 12s 0d indicating that he was reasonably prosperous. He was given no trade in his will and inventory, but was clearly both a grocer and a mercer, perhaps the forerunner of a general store keeper. The inventory makes clear that some of the linen cloth came from London, but he could also have bought supplies from the clothiers, kerseymakers and linen weavers in Charing and more widely in the Weald. Dubble is one of the few traders whose premises can be identified. He occupied the former medieval open-hall house at 52 High Street, on the corner of the cross roads and facing the market place (Fig. 3.4, Map 2.9). His inventory lists his possessions in his hall, buttery, kitchen and shop with chambers over and a workhouse at the rear. In addition to his shop goods he had barber's equipment in his kitchen and used the workhouse for making candles. Another wealthy grocer was Alexander Burwash. He died in 1662 with goods valued at £308 3s 2d, making his total the second highest among the tradesmen's inventories. He had a large house, including a warehouse where goods were stored, and in 1664 his widow was charged on six hearths.

There were no bakers in Charing at this date, which suggests that baking was done in the home, baked in ovens that were incorporated in brick chimney stacks. Of the butchers, Richard Rade had probably retired when he died in 1683. His goods were valued at only £38, but he had a large house with eight rooms and was charged on four hearths in 1664. Nicholas Baldock, a rippier (someone who transports fish inland from the coast) had equipment such as tubs, keelers and 'ripperees' (possibly fish baskets) in his shop in 1640, but there was no mention of fish.

Flour was probably supplied by local mills. The 1639 map of the Calehill estate labels 'windmill field' on a small hill south of Burleigh Road, on what is now the far side of the railway line. Pett may have owned a watermill near the present abattoir and sewage works. Filthes, Fills or Field Mill, on the river Stour at the border with Egerton parish (Map 1), is known from at least 1495 and was leased or sold several times during the seventeenth century. It was a watermill with two wheels, and in 1624 was referred to as a wheat mill and a malt mill. Another watermill lay further east at Newlands. This was owned by the Darells and was tenanted by one Samuel Reading in the early seventeenth century. Nothing about his work is known, although a small building over a stream to the north-east of Newlands, and a nearby house with a chimney were drawn on the 1639 map indicating the mill's location (Fig. 2.5). All the structures have long been demolished.

Charing was a good overnight stopping place for people travelling between east and west Kent. In 1686, a national survey of inns and alehouses itemised the numbers of guest beds and stabling for horses in each town. Charing, with twenty beds and stabling for fifty-two horses, plus three more beds and room for six more horses in Charing Heath, had half the provision of Ashford and a quarter that of Maidstone. None of the other villages on the main road, such as Lenham and Harrietsham, occur on the list at all.

By law, seventeenth-century travellers required passes, and the court baron of 1651 records them for eighty-three names, including the Hon. Lady Stannop, two baronets, four knights and eighteen gentlemen. Such people no doubt contributed to the economy of the town. The main inn was The Swan, now Elizabethan Court (Map 2.8), owned by the Honywoods of Pett as part of the manor of Charing. It was in the occupation of Thomas Padge in 1625 and Ralph Rasell in 1629. At its core was a medieval house with an open hall, but the hall was ceiled and the building greatly enlarged and enhanced in the seventeenth century (Figs 3.4, 7.19). Philip Lane, who died in 1673 with no stated occupation, was almost certainly a well-equipped innkeeper, and was perhaps a later landlord of The Swan. Downstairs he had a parlour, a hall with a little chamber next to it, a dining room with fourteen leather

Fig. 3.4 Richard Dubble's shop (52, 54 High Street), and The Swan Inn (58, 60, 62 High Street) (S Pearson)

chairs and two tables, as well as other chairs and stools. In addition there was a kitchen, buttery, brewhouse and a cellar containing ten barrels of beer. Among his goods were brass pots weighing 130lbs (the number of pots is not given), kettles of brass weighing 48lbs, wine pots, flagons, chamber pots and candlesticks of pewter altogether weighing 48lbs, and pewter dishes weighing 65lbs. Upstairs there were six named chambers, mostly with beds, including one called the Swanne chamber, two more beds in a passage, and three more in the garret. This accommodation surely supplied quite a high proportion of the twenty guest beds listed in 1686.

Other inns were the sixteenth-century King's Head, at the time known as The Three Bells, which was at the top of the High Street on the west side (Fig. 7.28, Map 2.40), and The Red Lion, where a riot took place in 1599 leading to a trial at Maidstone Quarter Sessions. This lay at the bottom end of the street, in the house now called The Firs (Map 2.23). Two licences for common alehouses or tippling houses had been issued in 1592 and 1594; the first was to Thomas Baylie for 'the sign of the Tiger in the chief street of Charing'. He must have kept a disorderly house for he lost his licence in 1600. The other was to William Spillett, who was also a butcher; he had a new house called 'the sign of the Crown'. As was common at the time, his licence contained a clause forbidding the playing of unlawful games such as tables, dice, cards, tennis, bowls, quoits and 'soggettes' (a game of throwing bones at a stick).

Miscellaneous

Licences to midwives were granted in 1634 and 1637. A Ralph Dubble, who may have been related to Richard the grocer, was licensed as a physician and surgeon in 1612, and 'chirurgeons', or surgeons, were present in the town throughout the century. One of them, John Hart, died in 1695 leaving 'a case of instruments and lancetts' and a 'case of scissors and razors and other things'. He was not only a barber-surgeon but had 'implements for chandlers use' in his workhouse.

House-builders in the town probably obtained bricks and tiles locally. Tile Lodge brickworks, possibly the successor of the medieval tile working discussed earlier, was on the sandy outcrop to the north-east of Charing Heath, and was by this time owned by the Darell family (Map 1). A couple of the tenants are known, one of whom, Thomas Simmons, was making bricks as well as tiles when he died in 1669. Tiles were the more valuable commodity: twenty-five loads of plain tiles being valued at £20, as against £15 for twenty-three loads of bricks. By this date new buildings in the parish were built of brick and most of the timber houses were having brick chimney stacks inserted. Simmons was a wealthy man with an inventory valued at £186. He lived in a large house of eight rooms; was charged on three hearths in 1664 and had a working farm of seventeen acres.

House furnishings improved during the seventeenth century. Wicker and rush seated chairs are first recorded in the parish in 1639 and old board bedsteads gave way to mat and cord bases after 1640. Fashions in clothing might alter, but as clothes were expensive, hats, gowns and petticoats were bequeathed and worn as they were or adapted. Gloves remained fashionable throughout the century, although shoes became more common than boots after 1660. No one in Charing was super wealthy, gentry being largely of local rather than county significance, but several of the traders and other parishioners were comfortably off. Most of the trades were practised throughout the century, and although the list of Charing traders illustrates the decline of the Wealden cloth industry, linen weaving held up rather better and remained important into the eighteenth century. The extent of the leather trade may be surprising, but this was possibly typical for the region since Ashford had a renowned cattle market and Faversham is known to have exported leather to London.

Education

In the second half of the sixteenth century there was considerable interest in education and a number of grammar schools were set up in the towns. Teaching in the countryside was much less well organised. By the seventeenth century there must have been some education in Charing for teachers are known to have been licensed there in 1607, 1610 and 1640, one of whom was Edward Draynor, son-in-law of Anthony Dering of Peirce House. When George Wheler, who was brought up in Charing, wrote his memoirs he refers to the fact that his father Charles, who lived in Charing manor house in the early seventeenth century, had a private tutor, who might even have been Draynor. George himself, born in 1651, says he was educated at 'bad schools' in Ashford and Wye, and later privately by the parish priest. In 1664 the churchwardens' accounts contain a single enigmatic reference: 'paid for letter about a schoolhouse, 6d', but whether anything came of this is not known. It is possible that there is much more to learn about education in the parish in the late seventeenth and eighteenth centuries. At present all we know is that when Elizabeth Ludwell, who lived in the fine early eighteenth-century Ludwell House in the High Street (Fig. 3.5; Map 2.39), died in 1765, she bequeathed £25 a year for 'a fit and proper person' to be employed to teach reading, writing and accounts to poor children in the parish, and that in 1794 a Mr Thomas Smith is known to have been appointed to the post. Even today the income from the Ludwell bequest is used to make small grants towards students' education.

Fig. 3.5 Ludwell House, High Street (A T Adams)

Relieving the poor

The problem of the poor was perennial. Until the mid sixteenth century almsgiving was common, but remained a personal matter. However, as the population rose, the issue became too acute for it to be left to chance and poor rates were established by law, with all wealthier people paying taxes to relieve the poor of their parish. Even so, by the end of the sixteenth century failed harvests, recurrent plague, high taxation (to pay for foreign wars), high food prices and rising inflation meant that many people, not just the sick and elderly, were reduced to penury. In many towns there were distributions of cheap corn to the poor in the 1590s. We have no firm evidence in Charing, but although the rural situation was probably easier than in towns, and in some cases wealthier relatives and neighbours no doubt helped those in need, things cannot have been easy. Despite the poor rates, several people still left money, corn or bread in their wills for distribution to the poor, and the situation was exacerbated by an influx of vagrants, migrants seeking work in the towns, and people trying to get home from war or other misfortunes, such as shipwreck. At this date references to them do not occur often in the churchwardens' accounts, but in 1601 a number of people who came through Charing from as far afield as Devon and Ireland, presumably without passes, were whipped and conveyed to an officer of the law to be sent back to where they came from.

At the beginning of the seventeenth century things may have eased a bit. As far as we can tell from the churchwardens' accounts, the poor rates were augmented in various ways. In 1607 a poor man's box was placed in the church for donations, the proceeds used to aid the old and infirm. In 1624 several wealthier inhabitants contributed towards the rent of a house for the poor, and several people, including Sir Robert Darell, helped the churchwardens with funds to get poor boys apprenticed. By the 1630s the churchwardens began paying small sums for the heads of vermin: 12d for a fox's or badger's head, 2d for a hedgehog, with the amount going up towards the end of the century. Polecats, stoats, magpies, crows and even sparrows were added to the list. Although these payments were never specifically linked to relieving the poor, it must have been a way by which a family could supplement its income. In the 1660s several poor widows, including Mistress Dering, formerly of Peirce House, received loads of firewood. In the 1670s the practice of providing abatements for rent owed became common.

But towards the end of the century, evidence of migrants in the churchwardens' accounts overshadows local problems. Nearly every entry in the churchwardens' books mentions alms given to people passing through Charing: men, women and children, blind, injured, or

Fig. 3.6 The junction of the High Street and School Road in the early nineteenth century. 47 High Street (Wady and Brett's) and Ludwell House are to the left. (CDLHS)

dispossessed by fire or other adversity. All these people had certificates or passes proving, or purporting to prove, that their situations were genuine. It is staggering to see how many people were helped. For example, in September 1670, nine seamen whose ship had been wrecked were collectively given 1s 6d. A few days later fourteen more arrived, and finally two companies passed through. Well over a hundred people received relief during that year. In June 1671 payment was given to nine seamen, then to two families of travelling people, followed by two women with children, ten seamen, and finally two merchants' widows. Once again the total for the year was well over a hundred, and it continued in this manner for the rest of the century. Some of the entries are particularly heart rending, such as 6d to 'a poor woman and her child who were laid down at my door'. The individual payments ranged from 6d to 2s (£4-£16 in today's currency), which means the strain on the parish, added to the cost of looking after its own poor, must have been considerable.

The Vestry was established in the sixteenth century as the governing body of the parish, and among its duties was administering poor relief. Unfortunately no vestry minutes for Charing are known before 1701, which is why the evidence for relief of the poor in the seventeenth century is so patchy. But from this date onwards there are agreements to provide money or rent, weekly, monthly or quarterly to various people in the parish, as well as help with clothes, shoes, fuel, medical expenses or house repairs. In 1718, £20 was given to the parish to be used towards building houses for the poor, and in 1719 a smith's forge on the parish plot was to be pulled down and almshouses built instead. The 1840 tithe map suggests that the parish plot was where 1 and 3 High Street are today, although the present building only dates to the early nineteenth century (Map 2.29).

Fig. 3.7 The Market Place, leading to the church and palace; Nethersole House is on the right (S Salter)

The Honywood and Sayer families of Pett

During the seventeenth century, the Honywoods were probably the nearest Charing came to residential gentry of relatively high status. Robert and Mary Honywood, who came to Pett in 1543, enlarged their home by adding a fine timber-framed wing which forms the front range of the present house, set behind a later brick façade (Fig. 3.8). They had sixteen children, and by the time of Mary's death in 1620, aged 93, she was reputed to have 367 descendants. Her grandson, Sir Robert the elder (knighted 1625), himself had several sons, the eldest of whom was Sir Robert the younger (knighted 1627), who had a distinguished career as a diplomat during the Commonwealth. He paid tax on twenty hearths at Pett in Highslade borough in 1664. Although he did not die until 1686 (when he was buried in Charing church, Fig. 3.9), he seems to have passed his property to his son, also Robert, during his lifetime. This Robert fought against the English in the second Dutch War and was attainted for treason in 1667; the estates were sequestered, and he died abroad sometime before 1673. However, the crown allowed the property to be held in trust for his widow and sons by two of his uncles, Sir Philip Honywood and Sir Henry Vane, and in 1673 Pett was bought by Sir Philip, who died there in 1685. His daughter and heiress, Frances, married George Sayer, MP for Canterbury in 1695 and 1702, who died in 1718 and is remembered in a monument in the church (Fig. 3.10). The Sayers remained at Pett until the twentieth century. George, grandson of the first George, became High Sheriff of Kent in 1755. His son, another George, was rector of Egglescliffe in Co. Durham, and was seldom in Kent. The fifth George settled at Pett and was Deputy Lieutenant for the county. He died unmarried in 1874 and the estate passed first to an unmarried sister, and then to his uncle, John. There were two further Johns and two Arthurs, the last of whom, who never lived at Pett, sold it in 1952.

Fig. 3.8   Pett Place, south front (A T Adams)

and equally large wash house, a flour room, dish room and potato room. Sundries listed included a spinning wheel and cards, six wheelbarrows, and many hoes, spades, shovels etc., suggesting the sort of labour the inmates had to do.

Between *c*.1500 and *c*.1800, the country experienced tremendous religious, political and economic upheavals, the effects of which can best be seen by following the fortunes of the local gentry, and noting the increasing numbers of poor that the parish had to cope with. But for the so-called 'middling sort', families who owned farms, or gained their livelihoods through craft or trade, the effects

Fig. 3.9 Monument in Charing church to Sir Robert Honywood the younger, died 1686 (S Pearson)

In 1766 Sir John Filmer's house (now The Old House in Station Road, Fig.7.17, Map 2.22) was to be repaired for the reception of the poor, and a husband and wife appointed to look after them. In addition, by 1796 the parish came to own Nethersole House, 1-4 Market Place (Fig. 3.7, Map 2.10). It was to be a workhouse, part of which was to be occupied by paupers for nothing, and part of which was to be rented. Exactly how the building was organised is not clear, but an inventory of the rooms and furniture within it made in 1835 was published in *About Charing*. It indicates that there was a master's house, twenty beds in seven dormitories, plus a tramp's room with nothing in it but a stove and two stools. There was a hall with tables, chairs and forms, a large kitchen

Fig. 3.10 Monument in Charing church to George Sayer Esq., died 1718 (S Pearson)

are much less clear. Such inhabitants appear to have been part of a self-sufficient community that provided most of what was needed from its own resources. Charing was linked to the outside world but from the sort of evidence available it would appear that people were relatively untouched by external events, and that there was little change over this long period. Whether this was truly the case is hard to say.

Fig.11 The Old Ashford Road looking west. Tanners Lodge is to the left; drawn by Horace Barwick, 1830s (CDLHS)

Chapter 4: Charing in the nineteenth century

by Stephanie Reed

Introduction

By the end of the eighteenth century the population of Kent, which had been largely static during the seventeenth and early eighteenth centuries, began to grow. This trend continued throughout the nineteenth century, despite downturns in the 1850s and 1860s. A substantial fall just before 1900 may in part be related to alterations to the parish boundaries when the modern civil parish replaced the ecclesiastical parish (Table 4.1, Map 1). Change was much more rapid in the nineteenth century than earlier, and this chapter looks at life in Charing mainly through studying the trades and occupations recorded in the ten-yearly census returns for the period between 1841 and 1891.

Table 4.1

The population of Charing parish in the nineteenth and twentieth centuries

Year	1801	1811	1821	1831	1841	1851	1861	1871	1881	1891	1901	1911	1921	2001	2006
Pop	851	912	1,103	1,237	1,241	1,321	1,258	1,298	1,349	1,314	1,170	1,223	1,207	2,284	2,694

In 1801 Kent was still a largely rural county and farming the most important activity. It is reported that 54,124 people were employed in agriculture, compared to 43,253 in trade and industry, and of over 51,000 labourers only thirty per cent were in non-agricultural work; the Charing ratios were similar to those of Kent as a whole. Farming was still mixed; corn and sheep predominated on the Downs to the north; cattle, corn and hops lay in the shallow valley where the main transport route and the town lie; and mixed agriculture, including fruit, was found on the sandstone ridge to the south of the parish. Many of the farmers were tenants of gentry estates, such as the Darells of Calehill and the Sayers of Pett Place.

A lot of the trades practised in the parish were connected to farming: saddlers, wheelwrights, leatherworkers, blacksmiths, and lime burners. Industrial trades found in the area were brick making, tile making and papermaking. The village was fortunate to have numerous shops to sustain the inhabitants and many trades to enrich village life. In the seventeenth century Kent had had a strong weaving industry but by the nineteenth century there were no more weavers in the parish, although the skill may still have been practised at home. The census information between 1841 and 1891 has been distributed between Tables 4.2-4.6.

1800 – 1840

During the first half of the nineteenth century the position of agricultural labourers deteriorated, despite the introduction of the Corn Laws of 1815, by which tariffs were imposed on cheap imported grain for the benefit of English farmers. Post-war inflation after the Napoleonic wars led to high rents and some farmers had to give up, resulting in vacant farms for which no tenants could be found, while others had to reduce their labour force. Combined with the demobilisation of troops, the results were widespread unemployment and a deep post-war depression.

Table 4.2
Agricultural trades and occupations in Charing from the nineteenth-century census returns

TRADES-OCCUPATIONS	1841	1851	1861	1871	1881	1891
Agricultural labourer	189	101	198	164	163	145
Carter			24	1		
Dairy maid [Farm servant]	0[2]	0[20]	1[-]	0[14]	0[7]	0[18]
Farmer's boy, Yardman		7	2	1	2	1
Farm bailiff			6	3	10	9
Farmer	26	23	22	24	26	31
Farmer/Grazier	1	1		3	1	
Farmer/Grocer				1	1	
Hay trusser				1		
Miller's loader		2		1		
Miller [Miller graziers] [Grinder]	5[-][-]	3[-][-]	4[2][1]	3[1][-]	3[2][-]	4[-][-]
Miller's asst [Miller's apprentice]		1[-]			0[1]	
Publican farmer					1	
Shepherd, Cowman		1	4	4	2	3
Waggoner [Waggoner's mate]		2[1]	3[2]			

In 1829-30 the situation was exacerbated by a bad harvest combined with a severe winter, and to make life worse a wet summer followed and the hop crop failed. Wages were low, conditions poor, and there was strain on the parish Vestry as so many poor people once again required assistance. In 1835 it was recorded that the parish owned its workhouse and poorhouse, Nethersole House at 1-4 Market Place (Fig. 3.7, Map 2.10), two cottages at 1, 3 High Street, and six cottages called the Barrack Houses on the road to Charing Heath. It would have needed all these and more to house the poor during these years.

Already in 1826, the Select Committee on Emigration had been told by Thomas Hodges of Benenden that every parish in the Weald of Kent had 'for some years past' suffered from surplus population and pauperism. In 1830 the appalling poverty led to the destruction of threshing machines, which, it was thought, were taking away labourers' jobs; the Swing Riots had started, named after a mythical figure called Captain Swing. Corn and livestock were stolen and highway robbery took place. Corn stacks and barns were burnt, and water pipes cut so that they could not be used, the actions being accompanied by letters to unpopular owners and occupiers threatening murder, arson and assault. Large bodies of labourers marched from parish to parish, coming at least as near to Charing as Lenham, demanding wages of 2s 3d a day in winter and 2s 6d a day in summer, a reduction of rent and fuel prices, constant employment and the increase of parish allowances for children. The Dragoon Guards were activated and gentlemen, tradesmen, watchmen and regular patrols were used to bring about peace. Executions, imprisonment and transportation followed. This did not end the problem, which continued in various forms until 1838. Despite this, tithes, whose abolition had been demanded during the riots, did not become a major issue when the Tithe Redemption Act of 1836 was passed. Instead of abolishing tithes altogether, annual payments 'in kind' were converted into an annual money charge based on the price of grain crops. Charing agricultural workers may have only been marginally involved in these problems, but the parish must have been affected as were others in the area.

In the nineteenth century voluntary associations for the prosecution of felons were formed across Kent to deal with crime. A Charing Society for Prosecuting Thieves had been established before the end of the eighteenth century. Its members had to reside locally and most of its work was of a fairly routine nature, but in 1799 a successful prosecution led to someone receiving a death sentence, commuted to life transportation. Since poverty still existed so did resentment, and in 1844 and 1846 a farm in Charing was burnt to the ground because 'much prejudice existed against a threshing machine which the farmer had at work'. Later, in the 1860s, the only misdemeanour in Charing which has been published was that of a labourer, Thomas Feakins, accused of using a terrier to hunt rabbits, no doubt to feed a hungry family. But there is probably much more to be found by searching the records.

The 1841 census

The census provided information on the resident population and visitors over a single day. The 1841 form, the first to provide individual details, was not as informative as the later ones since it did not show where people lived or worked, or give much information about names, gender, ages, family relationships, occupations, visitors, or where a person was born. It was taken on 6 June, and later censuses were moved back to March and April to avoid the summer and autumn movement of the population involved in the harvesting of hops, fruit, corn etc. As is well known, Londoners in particular came regularly to Kent for family working holidays.

Many people in the census would have had difficulty in stating their occupation as they often practised more than one. For example, shoemakers not only made shoes but sold them, bakers both baked and sold bread. There were those who practised two separate trades, miller and farmer, hairdresser and postmaster, and others undertook seasonal employment as a second money earner. The housewife probably made goods at home to sell, and undertook harvest work and other part-time work, all to help to bring more much needed money to the family. In 1803 it is recorded that a labourer was paid 2s to 2s 6d for a ten-hour day. For specialised work the rate was much higher: in 1803 the rate for hoeing, for example, was between 4s and 5s a day. Women, however, were paid much less: 6d to 8d for a day's weeding. By 1840 wages were greater, but for a ten-to-twelve hour day women still only received 1s and young boys 6d at harvest time. Children, even though described as scholars, often helped with the harvest, scared crows or collected windfalls.

The 1841 census shows twenty-six farmers in the parish employing 189 agricultural labourers and two farm servants. The agricultural workforce was hierarchical with two main categories of labourer: farm servants, such as ploughmen, waggoners, shepherds, carters and dairymaids, who were hired and paid by the year and often boarded in the farmhouse; and field labourers who were employed for only short periods of time according to the demands and needs of the farming season and who were paid by the task or by the hour, day or week. Within this tiered system wage levels varied considerably according to the worker's age, skill and gender.

Many children were sent as agricultural labourers at an early age which had an adverse effect on their education. Only three scholars were recorded in the 1841 census although, following from the will of Mrs Elizabeth Ludwell in 1765, a schoolmaster to teach poor children had been appointed at least by 1794. Where he taught is not certain, but the lack of scholars in the census may reflect the lack of instructions to parents when filling in the form as much as a lack of pupils in a school. The census recorded two schoolmasters, one schoolmistress and a teacher, although some of these may have been private tutors to the children of the gentry. Children were often required to contribute to their family's income as soon as they were able. Apprenticeships were few – in the census only a blacksmith, the sweep and the grocers had them, and these were often the children of the craftsmen and traders concerned. Other children were sent away as 'live-in' servants to earn money and reduce the strain on the family. Service was the second most common source of employment, with fifty-two people working as house servants in wealthier households.

Many traders were located in the centre of the town. Only two inns were named in 1841: The Swan in the High Street (Fig. 7.19, Map 2.8) and The Red Lion at Charing Heath. We know that others existed at that time, for example The King's Head in the High Street (Fig. 7.28, Map 2.40), but at this date they are not readily identifiable. Only one butcher was recorded in the village although it may not be a correct reflection of the actual situation. It is said that farmer's wives did much of the butchering, the meat being sold to a butcher for sale to the public. But Table 3.1 shows there had been butchers in the parish since at least the seventeenth century. If there was no one who butchered on the farm then a slaughterhouse would have been part of the butcher's shop. Sherborne House, 27, 29 High Street (Fig. 7.12, Map 2.35), was once a butcher's shop with a slaughterhouse and yard at the rear.

Changes that had taken place since the seventeenth century included the disappearance of the cloth industry, although there was still one weaver in the parish. New trades included a baker, suggesting less baking was done at home (Figs 4.1, 4.2), a clockmaker for the clocks that were now more widely available, a plumber to deal with installation of water systems in wealthier homes, also a hairdresser, a stationer and a pattern maker. As well as the grocers

Fig. 4.1 G Langford, Baker and Confectioner, at 21 High Street. Note the two horse drawn delivery carriages loading up to deliver their bread and confectionery. The area behind the property is now residential and known as Pilgrims Court (CDLHS)

Table 4.3
Household trades and occupations in Charing from the nineteenth-century census returns

TRADES-OCCUPATIONS	1841	1851	1861	1871	1881	1891
Butler, Steward		3	2	3	2	1
Cook, Pastry cook	1	2	5	5	1	8
Domestic servant		7	18	8	11	16
Gardener		2	6	9	7	9
Groom, Coachman		6	7	6	6	7
House servant m/f	52	34	36	25	39	17
Housekeeper		8	14	17	11	23
Lady's maid			1	1		
Nurse, House & Parlour maid		4	7	7	2	13

there was a fruit dealer, indicating the importance and availability of fruit from Kent orchards. The parish included three solicitors, two laundresses, and two post-boys to deal with the increasing amount of correspondence sent by road. In rural areas it appears that brick making was still taking place, as was burning of chalk by lime burners. The chalk was quarried from the Downs between Charing and Maidstone, and kilns near the quarries manufactured large quantities of lime that supplied much of the county with fertiliser. Welsh cattle still formed the most common stock of steers and milking cows in Kent; the drover would have brought them from markets in Ashford and Maidstone, and taken back those to be sold.

Fig. 4.2 G Lee, Grocer and Baker, 4 High Street. This is still a grocer's shop (CDLHS)

The 1851 census

In the ten years since 1841, census taking had become more precise and informative. The population had grown by nearly a hundred people. The number of farms had decreased slightly, and the number of farm workers was significantly down. Whether this meant that physical labour was being replaced by more mechanised horse-drawn machines is not evident from this source; possibly not, since in 1845 Kent farmers were reported to be conservative in their adoption of new farming methods. It is more likely to be primarily the result of a change in occupational classification or description since the number of agricultural labourers had grown again in 1861, while, in 1851, sixty-six people were described as general labourers compared to just two in 1841 and none in 1861 (Table 4.6).

By 1851 the total number of scholars had increased dramatically to 174. By this time parents were told to record children as 'scholars' if they were over the age of five and attending school or receiving tuition, but the large number noted also suggests that education was improving. By 1864 we know that Charing Boys National School had been established at what is now called Old School House, 64, 66 High Street (Map 2.7), and some of the five teachers and teaching assistants must have been working there. There are also occasional references to educating the girls upstairs.

The traders in the village show an increase in numbers since the last census. Five butchers are listed, although only two were in the High Street area, five grocers, and one man dealing in fruit. Horses were the main mode of transport and were still being used on the farm. The number of blacksmiths had doubled, while men in related trades were the two wheelwrights (Fig. 4.3, Map 2.5) and the two carriers. There was now a postmaster, the position combined

Fig. 4.3 The wheelwright at the Old Forge, 82 High Street: a major craft that served Charing well, making and repairing the wheels of agricultural vehicles and gentry carriages (CDLHS)

with a hairdresser, due to the increase in postal services, and new trades appeared such as a painter, a tin plate maker, a tea dealer, a watchmaker, and eleven dressmakers, a skill that women could do in their homes (although the term is sometimes said to have been a euphemistic way of referring to prostitutes). Several of these trades suggest there was increased wealth and leisure at least in some sections of society. Many people were still employed as household servants. The inns in the parish between them employed a barmaid, a housemaid, a cook, a bottler and several general servants.

The 1861 and 1871 censuses

Despite a dip in population numbers in 1861 the change was slight, and by 1871 the population was recovering again. Jobs in agriculture and the household remained the most common employment. For the first time there was a corn factor to deal with the sale of produce. Six men were termed millers or miller/graziers, the graziers probably acting as agents receiving and pasturing cattle until drovers arrived to take them to markets such as Smithfield in London. In the seventeenth century there had been two or three watermills in the parish: at Newlands and at Field Mill, the latter certainly working throughout the nineteenth century, and possibly one by the present abattoir. In addition there was a windmill at the end of Burleigh Road to the south of the village. In 1819 a three-storey smock-mill had been built on top of Charing Hill (Fig. 4.4). There were also three paper makers and several rag cutters who probably supplied them, but whether these worked at an unidentified mill in the parish or at one not far beyond the border, such as Batchelor's Mill in Little Chart, is uncertain.

It has been suggested that the late arrival of the railway to Charing and Lenham inhibited the development of industries in this area. But the line serving Ashford and Pluckley opened in 1842, and even though the railway did not come to the village until the 1880s its arrival in the vicinity did much to transform the parish. By 1847 Ashford was the largest industrial centre of East Kent, and a depression in farming in the 1870s meant that industries there were able to draw on cheap, unskilled labour. Charing was near enough to Ashford for people to take employment there for, as Harry Ward (1864-1940) described in his recollections of life in Charing in the 1870s, people thought nothing of walking the six miles to Ashford and back for work, school or pleasure. Despite the agricultural depression, the railway also meant that farmers were more easily able to get perishable produce to large markets like London.

Fig. 4.4 View of the windmill and mill house situated on Charing hill. The mill is now residential (CDLHS)

Table 4.4

Professional occupations in Charing from the nineteenth-century census returns

OCCUPATIONS	1841	1851	1861	1871	1881	1891
Accountant						1
Chemist's assistant			1		1	
General practitioner		1	2		2	4
Lawyer				1	1	
Magistrate		1	2	2	2	
Monthly nurse			1	2	2	1
Nurse	1	2	3	1	1	1
Parish clerk	1	1	1	1	1	1
Police constable			1	2	2	2
Solicitor	3	2	1	1	2	2
Solicitor's clerk		2	1	2	1	2
Surgeon [assistant]	3[-]	1[-]		1[1]	1[1]	
Vicar [Curate]	1[-]	0[1]	0[1]	1[-]	0[1]	2[-]

By 1871 there was a coal merchant in Charing, who presumably brought coal by cart from Ashford or Pluckley, and some of the four carriers listed might well have been employed by him. A lone engine driver perhaps worked for the South Eastern Railway Company from Ashford or Pluckley stations. Those who needed rapid transport but had no horse of their own could use the fly-driver, a one-horse, two-wheeled carriage, to take them to the railway and elsewhere.

Gas had arrived in Charing by 1871 and a gasworks manager was listed in the census. Harry Ward remembers that gas was used for street lighting and for better-off homes, everyone else still making do with rush and cotton wick candles, and later with paraffin lamps. In Charing town the number of occupations practised continued to rise. There were two police constables to keep order, and two magistrates and a lawyer resided in the parish. Two monthly nurses helped the medical practitioners, although the two general practitioners who were listed in the 1861 and 1881 censuses were for some reason missing from the 1871 census. The monthly nurse was someone with some training who attended women during the month after childbirth. The inns were doing well from travellers, and tradesmen and carriers were in demand running regular services for people to attend market days in Ashford and Maidstone. Town shop keeping changed as sources and supply grew, and hawkers, fairs and street markets were increasingly displaced by fixed shops.

Table 4.5

Educational occupations in Charing from the census returns

OCCUPATIONS	1841	1851	1861	1871	1881	1891
Governess		2	1	4	4	1
Pupil teacher		1	1		1	1
Scholars	3	174	218	218	284	277
Schoolmaster	2	1	1		1	1
Schoolmistress [Private]	1[-]	1[-]	2[1]	3[-]	3[-]	4[-]
Teacher [Teacher's assistant]	1[-]	1[1]	1[-]		1[-]	1[-]
Teacher - music and French						1
Teacher - music					1	1
Undergraduate					1	

Fig. 4.5 Charing school, 1872 (CDLHS)

Fig. 4.6 The school hall in 1895 (courtesy E Ellen)

One of the biggest changes in the parish was caused by the 1870 Education Act which stated that every village had to provide a school to be paid for from the rates. The ratepayers of Charing held a meeting of the Vestry on 17 November 1870, when it was proposed that property owners should subscribe the sum of 1s 6d in the pound of the rateable value, and the occupiers 6d in the pound, to cover the cost of a site and the erection of the necessary buildings. This was agreed, and Miss Charlotte Sayer, daughter of George Sayer of Pett Place, offered an acre of ground at the east end of Horse Lees in what is now School Road. The foundation stone was laid by Miss Sayer on 14 May 1872 and the school was opened on 13 January 1873 (Figs 4.5, 4.6, Map 2.38). A year later the lime trees that are still there today were planted. The price of education at that time was 3d per week for the first (highest) class and 2d a week for infants and other classes. Initially there were eighty-seven pupils, rising to 131 in 1879. In 1873 attendance was poor, the children were reported to be backward and

Fig. 4.7 Harvey House, 18 High Street, on the corner of the Old Ashford Road. This was a grocers shop owned by the Harvey family during the nineteenth century. In the 1871 census Robert Harvey, age 32, born in Chatham, a grocer and stamp dealer, resided in Charing High Street. He was married and had a four year old daughter, Lizzie. In the 1881 census Robert was called a master grocer, and lived in the Pluckley Road. His wife, Elizabeth, 41, was also born in Chatham. They had two daughters (Lizzie had died in 1871), both born in Charing and listed as scholars: Annie, 16, and Daisy, 10. By 1891 Elizabeth, grocer, had become head of the family. She had moved back to the High Street, and was perhaps living 'over the shop'. She was listed as born in Gillingham, perhaps because she had filled in the form more accurately than her deceased husband. Both daughters, now 26 and 20, lived with her. This photograph, taken around 1900, possibly shows a later picture of the Harvey family members and their staff. The building is certainly the property called Harvey House until recently (courtesy of Debbie Brett; CDLHS)

Fig. 4.8 Charing High Street, c.1910. It still looks very similar today, although fashions have changed and some properties are residential (CDLHS)

unpunctual, and it was noted that a number of absentees were employed rook keeping [sic] for members of the school committee. This sort of problem continued through the 1870s, for in 1878 the Attendance Officer who called to inspect the school found most of the children absent, at work in the fields. A typical example was Harry Ward who, in 1872 at the age of eight, went to work for the rope maker for two and a half days a week, rising to full time employment by the time he was ten.

The 1881 census

New specialised occupations continued to be recorded in the 1881 census, including a jeweller and a telegraph clerk. The number of agricultural labourers was very slowly diminishing, no doubt indicating the gradual introduction of farm machinery, and three traction engine drivers had appeared for the first time. Although the railway was not to arrive for another three years, the locomotive and carriage departments in the company's engineering works at Ashford provided opportunities to many, with large numbers of manual and administrative workers required for the day-to-day running of the passenger and freight services: station masters, engine drivers, footplate men, platelayers, linesmen, signalmen and booking clerks etc.; an engine driver, railway plate layer and signalman came from Charing.

Details of some establishments in the High Street provide vignettes into how certain businesses functioned. The owner of the Queens Head employed a beer retailer, a housekeeper, a coachman and a general labourer. The inn also took in lodgers, who at the time of the 1881 census were a grocer, a pupil teacher, a draper's assistant and a baker's assistant, the last three suggesting that young people were moving into the village to find employment. Similar staff and lodgers were to be found at the other three inns, namely The Swan (Fig.7.19, Map 2.8),

Table 4.6

Miscellaneous trades and occupations in Charing from the nineteenth-century census returns

TRADES-OCCUPATIONS	1841	1851	1861	1871	1881	1891
Baker [Master] [Asst] [Journeyman]	1[-][-][1]	0[2][1][1]	3[-][-][-]	1[-][2][-]	2[-][3][-]	6[-][1][-]
Baker/Confectioner				1	1	
Barber/Clog maker			1	1		
Barmaid [Barman]		1[-]	1[-]	1[-]	1[1]	3[-]
Basket maker	1	1				
Beer retailer [Beer retailer/Bricklayer]	1[-]	0[1]	1[-]	2[-]	2[-]	1[-]
Blacksmith [Asst] [Appr] [Journeyman]	3[-][1][-]	6[-][1][-]	5[-][-][2]	6[-][-][-]	4[-][-][-]	3[1][-][-]
Bookseller						1
Boot maker [Master]				1[-]	0[2]	0[1]
Bonnet maker	1					
Bottler		1				
Bricklayer [Master] [Labourer]	7[1][-]	2[1][2]	6[-][-]	1[-][3]	3[-][2]	2[-][3]
Brick maker [Brick/Tile maker]	3[-]	2[-]	1[1]	2[1]	3[-]	
Builder			1			3
Butcher [Journeyman] [Asst] [Appr]	1[-][-][-]	5[-][2][-]	3[-][2][-]	4[-][2][-]	5[-][3][1]	7[-][3][-]
Cabinet maker				1		
Carpenter [Master] [Appr] [Journeyman]	5[-][-][-]	2[4][-][2]	3[2][-][-]	5[1][2][-]	9[2][-][1]	7[-]][1][-]
Carpenter/Joiner [House] [Jobbing]			0[1][1]			2[-][-]
Carrier	2	2	2	4	3	3
Charwoman			6	1	3	3
Clockmaker	1			1	1	
Coal dealer [Merchant]				0[1]	1[-]	1[2]
Coalman [Coal warfe labourer]						1[1]
Cordwainer	1	1	2	3	2	
Corn factor			1	1		
Draper [Appr] [Asst]	1[-][-]	1[1][1]	2[-][-]	2[1][1]	2[-][2]	3[1][2]
Dressmaking trades [Asst]		11[1]	17[-]	11[-]	13[-]	6[1]
Drover	1					
Engine driver, rail [Fitter]				1[-]	1[-]	1[1]
Engine driver, thresher [Maker]			2[-]			0[1]
Fly driver				1		
Fruit Dealer	1	1		1		
Gamekeeper [Underkeeper]			1[-]	2[1]	1[-]	1[-]
Gas works manager [Gas maker]				1[-]		0[1]
Gatemaker / hurdles				1	1	1
General labourer	2	66	2	12	17	
General shop dealer [Asst]	1[-]	1[3]	2[-]	3[-]	3[-]	2[-]
Glover	1	1	1	1		
Greengrocer			1			
Grinder of cutlery					2	
Grocer [Master] [Appr] [Journeyman] [Asst]	4[-][4][-][-]	1[1][1][2][1]	2[2][1][-][3]	3[-][2][-][7]	1[4][-][-][6]	3[1][3][-][2]
Grocer/Baker [Grocer/Draper]		0[1]	1[1]	1[1]	0[2]	1[2]
Grocer/Tallowchandler [Grocer's Porter]		1[-]			0[1]	0[2]
Grocer shopman [Whoslm] [Warehm]		1[-][-]	1[-][-]	1[-][-]	0[1][-]	1[2][1]
Hairdresser [Master] [Appr]	0[1][-]	0[-][1]	1[-][-]		0[1][-]	1[-][-]
Hairdresser/Postmaster		1				
Handloom operator		1				
Harness maker			1			
Hawker - earthenware		2				
Hawker - tea and coffee		1		3		
Higgler			1			
Hoopbender [Hoopmaker]						1[5]
Innkeeper and Hostler	2	2	3	2	1	1
Jeweller					1	
Laundress	2	4	7	4	5	4
Limeburner [Limeburner/Woodman]	1[-]	2[-]		5[-]	5[-]	2[1]
Linen draper [Master]	1[-]	0[1]	1[-]			
Loader		1				
Maltster [Master]	2[-]	0[1]	2[-]			
Marine store dealer			1			

TRADES-OCCUPATIONS	1841	1851	1861	1871	1881	1891
Merchant clerk				1		
Milkman			1			
Milliner dressmaker [Milliner] [Asst]				1[-][-]	2[-][-]	
Mole catcher					1	
Ostler [Ostler/Horse clipper] [Groom]	1[-][-]		1[-][-]		2[-][-]	1[1][1]
Painter/Glazier [Painter/Paperhanger]		1[-]	4[-]			0[1]
Painter [Appr] [Journeyman] [Asst]				0[1][1][-]	2[-][-][1]	2[-][1][-]
Paper glasser, mill			1			
Papermill sorter [Papermaker] [Mechanic]		0[2][-]	0[3][1]		0[1][-]	1[-][-]
Pattern maker	1					
Plumber/Glazier Master [Plumber/Painter]		1[-]	0[1]	0[2]		0[1]
Plumber [Appr] [Labourer] [Asst]	1[-][-][-]		1[-][-][-]	1[-][1][-]	1[-][-][3]	1[1][-][-]
Pork butcher					1	
Postal rural [Boy] [Walking]	0[2][-]	0[2][-]		0[-][2]	2[-][-]	1[-][-]
Poulterer and Fish						1
Rag cutter [Rag/Bonedealer] [Sorter]			4[-][-]	2[-][-]		
Railway plate layer [Plateworker] [Labourer]					1[-][-]	2[-][9]
Railway porter [Signalman] [Stationmaster]					0[1][-]	2[2][1]
Rat catcher				1	1	1
Road man [Labourer]		1[-]		1[-]		2[1]
Rope maker [Journeyman] [Labourer]		0[1][-]		1[-][-]	2[-][-]	
Rough carpenter				2		1
Saddler [Journeyman] [Master]	2[1][-]	0[2][1]	0[-][1]		3[-][1]	
Saddler/Harness maker			1	1		1
Salesman						1
Sawyer				1		
Shoemaker [Appr] [Asst]	6[-][-]	7[2][-]	8[-][-]	5[-][-]	2[-][-]	4[-][-]
Shop boy [Errand boy]		1[4]				0[1]
Smith	1					
Spinner journeyman [Asst]	1[-]			0[1]		
Stamp distributor [Stationer dealer] [Asst]	0[1][-]	1[1][-]		1[2][-]	0[1][-]	0[1][-]
Steam plough/Lime merchant						1
Sweep [Appr]	1[2]	1[-]	2[-]	1[-]	3[-]	2[-]
Tailor [Tailor/Postmaster] [Journeyman]	5[-][-]	1[-][1]	3[-][-]	0[1][-]	3[1][-]	0[2][-]
Tailors' Appr [Servant] [Asst]		2[-][-]		1[1][-]	0[-][1]	
Tallow chandler [Journeyman]			1[-]			
Tea dealer		1				
Telegraph clerk [Letter carrier] [Messenger]			0[2][1]		1[1][-]	1[-][-]
Thatcher	1	2	1			1
Tilemaker [Tileman/Woodburer] [Labourer]			3[1][-]	4[-][2]	6[-][-]	4[-][-]
Tile burner				1		
Tin man			1	1		1
Tin plate maker		1			1	
Tobacconist				3		
Tollgate keeper	1		1	1		
Toy dealer/Maker					1	
Traction engine driver [Dealer]					3[-]	1[1]
Victualler	1	1	2	2	1	3
Watchmaker master [Appr] [Finisher]		1[-][-]	1[-][1]	1[-][-]	2[-][-]	2[-][-]
Weaver	1	1				
Wheel carpenter				1		1
Wheelwright [Journeyman] [Appr]	4[-][-]	2[-][-]	4[-][1]	4[-][-]	3[-][-]	1[1][-]
Wood dealer			2	1	1	

Abbreviations

Appr   Apprentice
Asst   Assistant
Warehm Warehouseman
Whoslm Wholesalesman

Fig. 4.9 The railway station (S Pearson)

The King's Head (Fig. 7.28, Map 2.40) and The Royal Oak (Map 2.30). Many of the traders, such as bakers, butchers, drapers, grocers, painters, tailors and the plumber, employed extra staff (Fig. 4.7). Apprentices were few and most of the staff were recorded as shopmen or assistants. Together with the lodgers in the inns, the picture is of far larger businesses than had been the case in 1841. Figure 4.8 illustrates the High Street and some of its shops at a slightly later date.

By 1884 the average attendance in the school was stated to be 157, considerably short of the 284 scholars recorded in the 1881 census (Table 4.5). The reasons are likely to have been the continuing problem of absenteeism, with parents known to record their children as 'scholars' even if they never attended school, and the presence of local private schools.

The 1891 census

The railway station in Charing was opened by the London Chatham and Dover Railway Company on 1 July 1884 (Fig. 4.9, Map 2.25). As a result more people were directly employed on railway business, which must have created welcome work for some local men, fewer than ever of whom were needed on farms. In the 1891 census there was an area marked as 'Railway Huts Station Road', which were probably in the Station Yard. The huts housed six families of railway plate labourers, who between them had twenty-two children. Ten children between the ages of five and eleven years were scholars, and one daughter was in service as a domestic servant. The railway also employed a stationmaster, two signalmen, an engine driver, an engine fitter, two porters, and three other labourers. Apart from the station master, who lived in Station House attached to the station, some of them lived in the High Street or in Old Ashford Road. In addition the coalman and coal wharf labourer may well have been connected to the railway rather than working for the coal merchant who had operated since 1871.

The coming of the railway meant that the coal merchant could now obtain his supplies without having to cart his wares from another station. It also meant that perishable goods for the shops would arrive at their destination in a better state, farm produce could be despatched more effectively, and cattle and sheep could be transported easily rather than driven by drovers to market. Possibly the grocer's porters were employed specifically to bring goods from the station to the grocer's warehouse where they were stored by the warehouseman. Older children could more readily continue their education in the schools of Ashford and Maidstone. On the other hand a possible adverse effect of the railway could be reflected by the fact that for the first time there were no brick makers listed in the census. It may be that the introduction of cheap bricks, moved by train from the north Kent brickfields, resulted in it no longer being economic to make them locally.

New, or relatively new, occupations in the parish included an accountant, a dedicated poulterer and fishmonger, a steam plough-cum-lime merchant, traction engine drivers, a telegraph clerk, and an increase in road menders. It would seem that Charing was slowly getting to grips with mechanisation, and that professionals and businessmen were able to move around the county more efficiently, whether by road or rail, and also maintain speedy communication with the outside world through the use of the telegraph. Nonetheless, there were still three carriers, and plenty of trades connected to the welfare of horses for riding and working. The point has been made that far from leading to the demise of horse traffic, the coming of the railways encouraged more travel generally. In particular carriers were useful for relatively local journeys because they could deliver goods to their actual destinations rather than depositing them at the nearest railway station.

Fig. 4.10 Charing Heath church, as completed in 1874 (J Grebby)

The development of Charing Heath village is particularly interesting in the later nineteenth century, for it had come from being a group of isolated farmsteads to a community proper. This was in no small way owing to the support and drive of the Sayer family of Pett Place who built the west part of the current church in 1861 to serve as an infants' school and chapel of ease. In 1868 the former heath was enclosed, and land granted to the Sayers was given by them for a church, school and vicarage, extending the original building to the east. The church of Holy Trinity was consecrated in 1874 and the present ecclesiastical parish of Charing Heath and Lenham Heath was created at the same time (Fig. 4.10).

In 1894 the Local Government Act was passed which established rural parish councils to undertake work previously overseen by the Vestry. The first elected councillors in Charing were the most prominent members of the community: the vicar, magistrates, landowners and shop keepers. Their duties were to look after the common land within the village for the good of the parish, to appoint overseers of the poor and raise funds to support the needs of the parish, and to acquire and maintain any necessary buildings needed for parish purposes, such as the parish hall which was built in 1897 on land purchased for £11 from Colonel Campbell (Fig. 4.11, Map 2.28).

At the same time the ecclesiastical parish of Charing was replaced by the civil parish. This meant that parts to north and south were lost to Stalisfield and Egerton, possibly contributing to a reduction in population, although a small area in the north was also gained. Westwell Leacon only became part of Charing in the 1950s. These changes have been marked on Map 1.

The censuses reveal the great changes that

Fig. 4.11 The parish hall, 1897 (S Pearson)

took place in Charing during the larger part of the nineteenth century. In 1841, despite being on the Ashford to Maidstone turnpike, with constantly passing horse traffic and good inns in the village, this was still a largely inward-looking agricultural parish. By the 1890s, the introduction of railways, farm machinery and the telegraph, as well as the increase in education, had turned it into a place no longer wholly dependent on agriculture, and its inhabitants looked outwards into the surrounding region. Communication of all kinds had become speedier; many people were employed outside the parish, while others even migrated in to work in the village which remained the commercial hub of the locality. Although the arrival of the automobile, the wireless and the telephone would make massive changes to people's lives during the twentieth century, the foundations of modern Charing were already in place by 1900.

charing christmas lights III

Fig. 5.1 Church of St Peter & St Paul from the south west (S Pearson)

Chapter 5: The Church of St Peter and St Paul

by Brian Easton

Introduction

The parish church of St Peter and St Paul (Fig. 5.1) lies to the east of the Market Place which itself is bordered on the north side by the archbishop's palace. The manor of Charing is recorded as a possession of the see of Canterbury from the eighth century, and like many of the other archiepiscopal residences, for instance Croydon, Lambeth and Maidstone, the buildings were placed close to the church. There was probably a church on the present site from the eighth century, although Domesday Book, which was completed in 1086, does not make any reference to a church in Charing. It was, however, listed in Domesday Monachorum, a Domesday related text. No evidence survives of what this church might have been like but the Monachorum record shows that Charing was a mother or minster church paying high dues to Canterbury. Originally it probably had several 'daughter' churches, although by Domesday only Egerton was listed (see p. 6).

The first Norman archbishop of Canterbury was Lanfranc, 1070-89, and he formally divided the church's possessions between those held by the archbishopric and those held by the cathedral priory of Christ Church. He retained Charing for the archbishop. The manorial system set up by the Normans meant that Lanfranc became lord of the manor of Charing, and so it remained for nearly 500 years with each succeeding archbishop until 1545. The archbishop created a number of subsidiary manors within the Charing estate and several of these – Newlands, Burleigh and Pett – built their own small stone chapels, among which a fine twelfth-century building remains at Newlands (Fig. 2.4).

It is possible that there was a stone parish church by or shortly after the Conquest, but there is no evidence of tufa or Caen stone remains such as might indicate an eleventh- or twelfth-century stone building. Perhaps the dispersal of Charing's daughter churches and manorial holdings resulted in there being few wealthy tenants able to contribute to building a fine stone church at that time. At any rate, the form and material of the church prior to *c.*1200 is unknown, although like other minster churches it may have always had a cruciform shape, but with a shorter chancel than at present.

The thirteenth-century church

The earliest surviving architectural evidence for the building dates to the late twelfth or early thirteenth century (Fig. 5.2). At that time the present nave and chancel, largely built of flint, were constructed, as indicated by two lancet windows on the north wall of the chancel and one on the north wall of the nave. Remnants of a sill and jamb which are probably from two other lancets survive on the south side of the nave, beneath and beside the later medieval windows. Previous historical accounts have said that the transepts were later, but although the piers defining the crossing are modern and the chamfered arches above only date to the fourteenth century, a roll-moulded string course beneath the east window of the north transept can only be of thirteenth-century date, indicating, as the outline of the plan suggests, that the chancel, nave, crossing and transepts were all built at one time. None of these parts of the church has an external plinth, distinguishing them from the later additions.

Professor Peter Kidson, an expert in the design of church buildings in Europe and the Middle East, has studied the church plan and concluded that there is enough evidence to show that the thirteenth-century building was designed by a properly trained architect, probably from the Canterbury masonic staff. What makes this likely is the choice of dimensions and the relations between them, plus the extremely high level of care taken in the setting out.

At 30m (100ft) in length this was by no means a small church, but it is highly unusual for its size and status in never having had aisles added to the nave. This may be a reflection of the lack of late-medieval wealth in the parish since the parishioners would have been expected to contribute to the provision of nave aisles which were often added to contain altars and images supported by the laity.

In the chancel is a plain piscina (inbuilt basin and drain for washing communion vessels) with a two-centred head which possibly dates from the original building of *c*.1200. To its west there is an elaborately decorated triple sedilia (seating niches for clergy) dating to the late nineteenth century. In 1852 Hussey reported that two of the three original seats had been partially filled up, and in 1854 they were described by Glynne as 'three plain rude sedilia, mishapen and obtuse'. This suggests that a plain thirteenth-century triple sedilia may have been rather inaccurately restored; but of this we cannot be sure.

Fourteenth-century alterations

In the early fourteenth century more light was required and in common with churches everywhere large new windows replaced some of the single lancets. The most striking of them is the square-headed window on the south side of the nave with four lights surmounted by a complex pattern of trefoil, quatrefoil and cinquefoil tracery (Fig. 5.3). Two simpler windows of similar style were introduced into the east and west walls of the north transept. Other late-medieval windows were inserted into the chancel, nave and transepts.

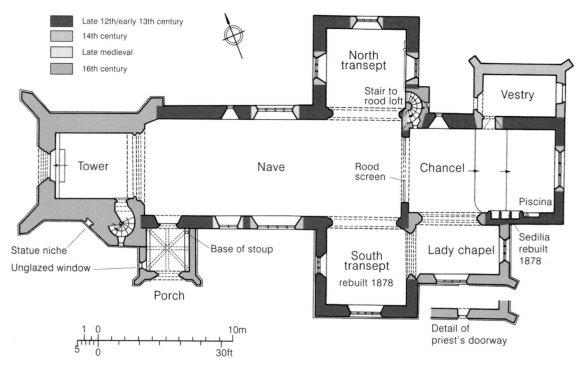

Fig. 5.2 Plan of the church in 2011 (A T Adams)

It is possible that during the thirteenth or fourteenth century a Lady Chapel was added to the cruciform church, perhaps in the position of the present Lady Chapel in the angle between the chancel and the south transept. In 1414 Henry Colbache, vicar, asked to be buried in the Lady Chapel. Although it has been suggested that this referred simply to an altar in one of the transepts, the fact that vicars usually requested burial in the east end rather than in the transepts, and that Colbache mentions a chapel and not just an altar, could indicate that it was an addition forming a chancel aisle, as so frequently occurred in the thirteenth and fourteenth centuries. In 1505 John Brent asked to be buried before the door of the 'new' chapel of St Mary so the two pieces of evidence together may indicate that there was an earlier, perhaps smaller, Lady Chapel on the site of the present one.

Fig. 5.3 Fourteenth-century square-headed window on the south side of the nave (S Pearson)

The vestry is a ragstone addition to the chancel, as indicated by the straight joint between the two, seen on the exterior of the east wall and the fact that it blocks one of the original lancet windows. It is, however, medieval in origin, although much altered. Indeed, the mere fact that it blocks a lancet window of *c*.1200 could indicate that the addition was made before other windows in the church were enlarged in the fourteenth century. It has a sloping roof, known as a catslide, of seventeenth-century construction, but a corbel in the north side of the north wall of the church probably remains from an earlier, lower roof also arranged as a catslide. In 1878 some changes to the vestry were proposed when other major work in the church was carried out, but this probably never took place, for in 1884 further alterations were drawn up, with a new traceried east window and elaborate fireplace. The churchwardens' minute book records a visitation by the Rev. Tindall, Rural Dean, on the 17 October 1894 and states that the church was in excellent repair, the vestry had been very carefully restored and all else was in good order. There is no record of what was done to the vestry, but there is no window tracery and only a small, plain fireplace, suggesting that the 1884 scheme was replaced by a simpler one.

The late fifteenth and early sixteenth centuries

In the late fifteenth and early sixteenth centuries there was a burst of new building activity in the church. This included the erection of the west tower, the replacement of the Lady Chapel on the south side of the chancel, the addition of the porch on the south side of the nave and the rebuilding of the rood loft.

The major internal alteration was the rebuilding of the Lady Chapel east of the south transept. It was originally known as the Brent Chapel or Chantry, after William and Amy

Fig. 5.4 Lady Chapel and priest's doorway from the south (S Pearson)

Brent who lived in Peirce House and funded its construction at the end of the fifteenth century. William died in 1496 before it was finished, but in his will he asks to be buried next to the tomb of one Roger Rey, and that the profits on certain of his land holdings be used 'to performe my wille as well in makyng of my chappell'. No details of the location were given and it is not known if he was buried there, but when his brother John died in 1505 he asked to be buried 'before the door of the new chapel of St Mary' so it seems that the Brent Chantry had been built by then. It can reasonably be assumed that Amy Brent was buried there when she died in 1516 for in her will she requested that she be 'buried within the Chapell of Our Lady of my owne edification within the church of Charyng'.

The new chapel is built of Kentish ragstone and has hollow-chamfered piers and arches on the north and west sides which are quite different to the straight chamfers of the crossing arches. The wide archway between the chancel and the chapel is four-centred, and was described by Glynne in 1854 as 'Tudor-shaped'. The south and east windows are also of early sixteenth-century date, but the timbers of the roof above were replaced a hundred years later. There is a small doorway under the window in the south wall (Fig. 5.4), which gave the priest and verger direct access to the chancel. At the Reformation, the chantry was suppressed, but rights and responsibilities towards the chapel remained, and these passed by marriage from the Brents to the Derings, and later to the Bulwer family of East Dereham in Norfolk. In 1878 they still had a legal interest in what was by then called the Wickens Chapel.

At much the same time the rood loft was repaired and refurbished. It is not known when a rood was first introduced, or the date of the stair up to the loft, which is set in a turret projecting in the angle between the chancel and the north transept and reached by a doorway in the east wall of the transept. Since the loft has gone and this doorway is blocked up there are no architectural details by which to date it. Roods are known from the thirteenth century and there may have been a simple screen and beam with a crucifix above at Charing, but the majority of surviving rood lofts date to the fifteenth or early sixteenth century. The lights of the 'Holy Cross' are first mentioned in wills from the late 1450s (this date is probably not significant since it is only from this time that wills start to survive), and the lights of the 'High Cross' occur from the 1480s. In 1496 there was a small bequest to the 'Blessed Mary of the Beme'. But in 1510 money was left for new building and making of the rood loft, although the Visitation of 1511 shows that it had not started, and later bequests for making, painting and gilding the rood loft and its images continued until 1527. Thus it is possible that an earlier beam with a crucifix and images was replaced in the early sixteenth century by a full-scale rood loft and more elaborate images and lights, including an image of St Thomas set in a tabernacle. Thomas Gibson, in 1518, requested his executors to gild the image of St Thomas in the rood loft 'and the tabernacle that he standeth in', and in 1527 John Geffrey left three shillings and four pence for the painting of St John in the rood loft. The stair to the loft can be seen through a small window high-up in the north wall of the chancel; this shows that the doorway from the stair emerged behind the monument above the present pulpit, indicating that the sixteenth-century loft lay in front of the chancel arch and not within it as the modern screen does. The wills referred to above also contain bequests to the altars of the Blessed Virgin Mary, the Holy Trinity and All Saints, as well as to the lights of some twenty saints kept permanently illuminated with candles given by parishioners.

Externally, the ragstone tower and porch were added during this period. The west tower was first mentioned in 1467 when John de Hache left £20 'to the work of the new tower if it be begun within seven years after my death'. In 1479 a further £10 was bequeathed for the 'new bell tower if my son dies' and in 1480 five marcs (13s 8d x 5) was to be paid annually for work on the tower 'when expedient'. This might indicate that the tower was still in the planning stage and hardly begun, but if so it probably started soon after for there were regular donations to the bell tower or steeple (the generic medieval term for a church tower and not the modern term for a steeple on the top) over the next sixty-five years, ending with donations for windows, floors and doors between 1536 and 1545. Thus its construction was a major task, paid for over many years by the parishioners. The five-storey tower (Fig. 5.1), with huge angled buttresses and an octagonal stair turret rising above roof level, is typical of Kent and particularly of this part of the county. Other nearby examples can be seen at Egerton, Lenham and Harrietsham, although Charing is one of the largest. Above the west doorway a traceried west window helped to light the nave; small windows lit the ringing chamber and clock chamber, while simple unglazed windows of three lights occur in each face of the bell chamber at the top. A fine west doorway with rich mouldings to the jambs and quatrefoils in the spandrels was under construction in 1536. The wall between the tower and the stair turret contains an external niche of curious form. It is assumed to be a statue niche, and presumably this is what it was, but inside the opening the niche is splayed outwards like a doorway, rather than curving inwards as is usual with a statue niche. It is also in a highly unusual position for an external statue but was probably put here to face people coming from the village to the main doorway on the south side of the church.

The south porch was added at the same time as the tower. It was not an integral part of the tower project, separated from it by a straight joint and with different doorway and plinth mouldings, but it was more or less contemporary and was finished by 1527 when John Geffrey bequeathed money for finishing the paving and requested burial, with a brass, inside the porch. The porch is spanned by an octopartite vault (the only vaulting in the church), which was originally coloured. The vault is carried on shield-shaped corbels with crenellations to the stone wall plate, and it has stone benches to either side, one of which has a column base which may have held a holy water stoup (Fig. 5.5). A little unglazed quatrefoil window faces west. The entrance arch is richly moulded, with vine scrolls between the inner and outer mouldings and quatrefoils in the spandrels above. These are no longer very distinct owing to severe weathering. There is a room or parvis above the porch accessed by a door off the tower stair. The roof above is flat and was leaded until recurring theft in the twenty-first century forced the churchwardens to use a lead substitute.

Fig. 5.5 Interior of south porch with porch doorway, vaulting and a base for a holy water stoup (S Pearson)

Grove records that the 1467 will of John at Hache mentions the making of two 'handbellys' and according to an inventory of church goods in 1552 Charing had four bells in the steeple, a Sanctus bell, and two handbells. There is no evidence to indicate whether these were the same two handbells. The Sanctus bell probably hung in the opening above the chancel arch. All the bells were lost in the 1590 fire but enough metal was recovered to cast a single bell which Stahlschmidt says bore the date 1608. It was probably made by Joseph Hatch.

The Reformation

The 1552 inventory, which was taken after the first wave of reform under Edward VI, reveals that a chalice and pax, which were no longer required, had been sold to John Brent; that the vicar had paid for the 'wrytting of Godys Word in our cherche', almost certainly the painting of texts on the walls so that those of the congregation who could read, could read them for themselves, and for a 'newe boke', presumably in English. Shingles and nails had been purchased and the roof had recently been re-covered. At this time one would have expected all altars except the high altar to have been removed and the rood to have been taken down. Then in 1557, under Mary, the church was visited by Archdeacon Harpsfield in a tour of

Kent churches to see what needed to be done to return the church to Catholic worship. The parish was told to restore various items, including providing a convenient place to set the images of St Peter and St Paul at the sides of the main altar. Since the previous pax had been sold, they were also to produce a pax of latten, i.e. a tablet of brass or similar material with the image of the crucifix on it which communicants kissed during the administration of Holy Communion. Various vestments and altar cloths were to be improved, including providing a cloth for the side altar, and 'a vele and a clothe for the roode agaynste Lent'. This confirms the existence of a side altar and that the rood had either not been removed or had been restored in the four years since Mary succeeded to the throne in 1553. After Mary's death the position will have been reversed again and the rood was almost certainly destroyed, but for this we have no documentary evidence. A new screen and rood was erected as a memorial to the fallen in the 1914-18 war.

The south transept is sometimes known as the Burleigh Chantry. Sir John Sayer of Pett Place wrote an account of the history of Charing church in which he recorded that Hasted had claimed this was so, but Sayer thought it more likely that when the chantry adjoining Burleigh manor house was suppressed at the Reformation, the owners acquired in substitution certain rights in the south transept of the parish church. The occupiers of Burleigh Farm retained the right of sitting in the south transept, and after the fire of 1590 Sir John Darell of Calehill, as lord of the manor of Burleigh, restored the seats in the transept.

The fire of 1590 and the rebuilding

In 1590 disaster struck. Robert Honywood who lived at Pett Place wrote a contemporary account known as 'The Honywood Evidences' and that is probably the most reliable record:

> 'Ye parish church of Charing was burnt uppon tewesday ye 4 of August 1590, and ye bells in ye steeple melted with ye extremyty of ye fier. Nothing of ye church was left but the bare waulls, except ye flower (floor) over ye porch, and flower over ye turret wher the wethercock doth stand. The fier chanced by means of a birding peece discharged by one Mr. Dios, which fired in ye shingells, ye day being extreme hott and ye same shingells very dry.'

There is little sign of damage to the stonework, although it has been pointed out that pink discolouration to the stones at the bottom of the great west tower arch is typical of ragstone that has been subjected to intense heat.

The new nave roof was built by the parishoners in record time and is dated 1592 (Fig. 5.6). On the exterior, the gable of the previous roof, steeper and probably of crown-post construction, can be seen against the church tower (Fig 5.14). The replacement, with a shallower pitch, is of butt side-purlin form. It has two rows of purlins or longitudinal timbers butting the principal rafters, tiebeams, carved brackets to collars and a single row of windbraces above. The principal rafters, tiebeams and collars are painted with an unusual scroll design in white or grey on black. The last pair of brackets against the crossing carries the date: on the left side '1592' and on the right 'ER 34' signifying the thirty-fourth year of the reign of Elizabeth I. The chancel was the responsibility of the lay rector, who was probably the Dean and Chapter of St Paul's Cathedral, who at that time held the advowson. Here a similar roof was built, but it took twenty-eight more years to complete, in 1620. The date is inscribed on the bracket over the east window.

Fig. 5.6 Nave roof of 1592, rebuilt after the fire of 1590 (CDLHS)

In both the nave and chancel the common rafters between the principals, and all the roofs above the tops of the collars, have at one time been concealed by lath and plaster, nail holes for the laths being clearly visible. This would have left only the painted surfaces visible. While this may have taken place later (as has no doubt been assumed), the way in which only the painted surfaces were exposed leads to the question whether this was in fact part of the original design. A drawing in the possession of the History Society shows clearly what the roofs looked like with plaster ceilings (Fig. 5.7). Unfortunately it is not dated but must have been drawn after 1766 because a memorial of that date to the left of the north transept arch is shown; while one which was probably erected in the late 1760s to the right of the chancel arch is not. A further impression of the roofs with plaster ceilings can be seen in the Lady Chapel, which was provided with a simpler version of the same butt side-purlin roof using precisely the same mouldings as those in the nave. No evidence exists as to when the lath and plaster work was taken down.

The seventeenth century

Furniture

The seventeenth century was largely devoted to restoring the goods and ornaments lost in the fire. The churchwardens' accounts record that in the late 1590s a new pulpit was supplied by Thomas Kynde at a cost of 34s. Chris Currie, who studied the early church furniture, considered that this must have been a significant piece of work, but sadly it was remodelled and then replaced in the 1630s. The accounts record work by William Amiss (also Amesse, Amys) who spent two days altering Kynde's pulpit for which he received payment of 3s 1½d.

Fig. 5.7 Nave showing roof before late 1760s, with rafters hidden by lath and plaster ceiling (CDLHS)

Fig. 5.8 Box pews and high pulpit in the nave, 1840 (J Owen)

Fig. 5.9 View of high pulpit from the Lady Chapel in 1841 (J Owen)

Seven years later Amiss was paid £5 to replace the pulpit completely, although there is no indication why this was necessary. Two prints, dated 1840 and 1841, show a very high pulpit with a sweeping curved staircase and this is presumably the same one (Figs 5.8, 5.9).

In the early seventeenth century pews were probably introduced for the first time, and a number with carved bench ends were made. These are currently located in the south transept in front of the organ and under the tower. The ends have carved heads which have been described as poppy heads or perhaps more correctly as heraldic lilies. They also have carved panels below, mainly with foliage, but three incorporate heads of 'green men', a medieval symbol of the spirit of the woodlands (Figs 5.10, 5.11).

The church purchased a communion table in 1624 for the sum of 12s; it is probably the one now standing in the Lady Chapel. The frame is made of elm and the top of oak. The name of the maker is not recorded but Currie considered it unlikely to have been made by one of the named craftsmen and probably bought from a joiner from outside Charing.

The original church chest was lost in the fire together with its valuable records. In 1594 the churchwardens bought a replacement and Currie described this as the oak chest with metal strapwork, probably made by Thomas Kynde who later made the pulpit. In 1635 another chest was purchased for 20s. It had three locks and keys but no maker was named. It is not of very high quality and Currie has identified the timber as an assortment of hardwoods: elm, walnut and oak.

There are several entries in the churchwardens' accounts relating to the provision of a new font. The first was in 1600, but there is some confusion because later entries in 1630

Fig. 5.10 Carved pew end showing 'green man'
(S Pearson)

Fig. 5.11 Carved pew end showing 'green man'
(S Pearson)

suggest that a new font was installed then. It must be assumed that the first font was replaced for some reason not recorded. In 1744, according to the Vestry minutes, a new cover was provided.

The Royal Arms

The Royal Arms, which now hang on the north wall of the nave opposite the south door, were also purchased in the seventeenth century. There has been considerable controversy over which king they represent. In 1621 (James I) James Cooper was paid 26s. for the King's Arms and the Ten Commandments. In 1664 (Charles II) Thomas Rogers was paid five guineas for drawing and painting the King's Arms and for this a frame was made by William Amys at a cost of £1.13s.6d. However, these Arms also seem to have been replaced since infra-red photography in 1990 confirmed that the faint '1635' (Charles I) was in fact '1685', the year that James II came to the throne. The present arms bear the date 1716 and appear to be the earlier James II Arms modified to meet the Hanoverian requirements of George I who succeeded in 1714. The Arms were subject to major restoration in 2009.

Church goods

The church is not particularly well endowed with plate. The most significant item is a steeple cup, so called because the domed lid has a tall spike on it reminiscent of a church steeple (Fig. 5.12). It is silver gilt with London hall marks of 1599; the whole body, stem, foot and lid, are decorated with scallop shells. It was the gift of Elizabeth Ludwell and is on permanent display in the Treasury of Canterbury Cathedral. A silver flagon with London hall marks of 1705 is the only other item of significance. Its origins are not known.

A rare possession is the vamping horn, probably dating from the seventeenth century and believed to be only one of eight surviving examples in this country (Fig. 5.13). It is in effect a very large megaphone made from soldered tinplate. Vamping horns can be as long as 8ft (2.4m), although the Charing example is only 5ft (1.5m) long with a mouthpiece. They were used to amplify the sound of the choir in church or to supply a missing part to the church band, and also to amplify the voice, for instance in making public announcements from the church tower. Also dating from the seventeenth century are the two splendid brass chandeliers, one in the nave and one in the chancel. They are known as Kentish Spiders but their origin is not known.

Clocks and sundials

In the words of Chris Williams, Charing is blessed with an abundance of evidence concerning its church clocks. The first clock was procured in 1627 but was only installed ten years later. It is known as a birdcage clock because of its cage-like construction. This was before nuts and bolts were available and wedges were used to brace the structure. It had only an hour hand. The clock was initially wall mounted above the pews and it was not until 1656 that it was transferred to the tower and an external dial acquired.

Fig. 5.12 The steeple cup (CDLHS)

Fig. 5.13 The vamping horn (S Pearson)

It was unreliable and costly to maintain, and in 1817 it was subjected to a major rebuild, when a minute hand was added. By the twentieth century it was clear that it had to be replaced and in 1910 a new clock was procured from John Smith & Sons of Derby. Charing's old clock was completely forgotten until 1970 when it was discovered in pieces in an outbuilding of the archbishop's palace by T R Robinson, a distinguished horologist. A clockmaker living in the village, Ken Stocker, undertook a complete restoration and once in working order it was mounted for display in the north transept. It was transferred to its current location under the tower as part of a major restoration in 1992.

There are many references in the churchwardens' accounts to the maintenance of a sundial, the earliest being in 1617. The wording suggests that the dials were made of wood and painted, although Chris Williams points out that the purchase of a 'Dyall' was probably a very accurate brass sundial used for setting the church clock. Although, as church clocks became more reliable, the need for a sundial became less significant the wooden sundial appears to have been maintained and the accounts show that it was repaired in 1828 and completely renovated in 1883. Early twentieth-century documentation confirms that the sundial was mounted above the south porch arch where it is today. It was then a square wooden board painted black with gilt lettering and bearing the mottoes 'Life's but a Shadow. Redeem the Time. Tempus Fugit'. It was periodically restored throughout the twentieth century and finally replaced in 1990 with a sheet metal face painted white with black lettering. The original mottos have been retained.

The eighteenth and nineteenth centuries

There is a paucity of information in the church records covering these two centuries, the eighteenth century in particular. The 1840 drawings show that during that century box pews had largely replaced the earlier free-standing ones. In addition it is likely that a western gallery was added. The drawings, done from the west, do not show the position of the gallery under the tower, which was accessed from a doorway in the tower staircase. The doorway has been sealed but the frame can still be seen quite clearly. Glynne saw the gallery in 1854 and described it as being in front of the tower arch and containing an organ. He said it was built in 1733, but gave no authority.

Little else of significance is known to have happened in the eighteenth century and it was not until the nineteenth that major changes took place. In 1874 the rural dean upheld a complaint from the churchwardens that a reredos had been erected behind the altar by mistake without consultation or a faculty. It appears that Miss Sayer of Pett had left a bequest in her will to pay for its installation. Responsibility for the execution of this gift had been assumed by the lay rector for the chancel, presumably the Dean and Chapter of St Paul's Cathedral, and the work had gone ahead without the agreement of the parish. This appears to have created quite a furore, the problem stemming from having a non-resident vicar and an unsuitable curate. The situation was only resolved with the arrival as curate of Bishop Tufnell, a retired bishop of Brisbane (the parish showed a curious anomaly at that time because a non-resident priest was vicar while a former bishop was curate-in-charge). There was reason to hope that the parishioners would be satisfied with the reredos if the Commandments, Lord's Prayer and Creed were placed in the chancel on each side of the east window. However, it is not clear whether the biblical texts were ever painted on the east wall and the reredos appears not to have been held in high regard, for in the mid twentieth century the incumbent took a hammer and chisel to the marble structure, apparently with the intention of trying to remove it! He did not get beyond chipping one corner so decided to cover it with canvas pasted to the surrounding wall and painted white. So it remained until the early twenty-first century when it was uncovered and the damage repaired.

Apart from routine activities covered in archdeacons' visitations, the most significant events concern the rebuilding of the south transept and a major restoration in 1878. The first recorded evidence is contained in the Vestry minutes for the 12 August 1812 in which it was agreed that the repair to the church should be as follows: that the south wing, now pulled down, should be erected again on the same site except that the roof should be a pitched roof and tiled with a parapet wall round the same instead of a flat leaded roof as before. This poses something of a quandary because drawings of the 1830s show a south transept with a flat roof and crenellations (Figs 5.14, 5.15). Hussey stated that 'the south transept was enlarged AD 1812, when the wall was faced with bricks'. Glynne stated in 1854 that the 'south transept is of brick and bad', and during a visitation by the rural dean in April 1864, it was recorded that 'the parishioners should agree to rebuild the south transept'. He repeated his remarks in 1868 and 1870, and in 1872 Archdeacon Harrison visited and said the south transept should be rebuilt in a style more in keeping with the rest of the church, recommending co-operation between the parishioners, the diocese and the Church Building Societies.

On the 25 April 1878 the Vestry minutes record that the churchwardens were asked to obtain a faculty for the restoration and reseating of the church according to plans drawn up by J P St Aubyn, architect, 'including taking down the western gallery and removing the organ to a more convenient situation, the restoration of the south transept and the placing of a peal of bells in the tower'. The final faculty states that 'in carrying out the said works it is intended also to alter the position of the font and prayer desk and to add a lectern as is shown in the said plans and to put the pulpit on a new base'. The faculty was submitted by the curate, Bishop Tufnell.

Fig. 5.14 *View of the church from the south-east showing the south transept with a flat crenellated roof; drawing by F Turner, 1834 (Private collection)*

Fig. 5.15 *View of the church from across the fields to the east; early nineteenth century (CDLHS)*

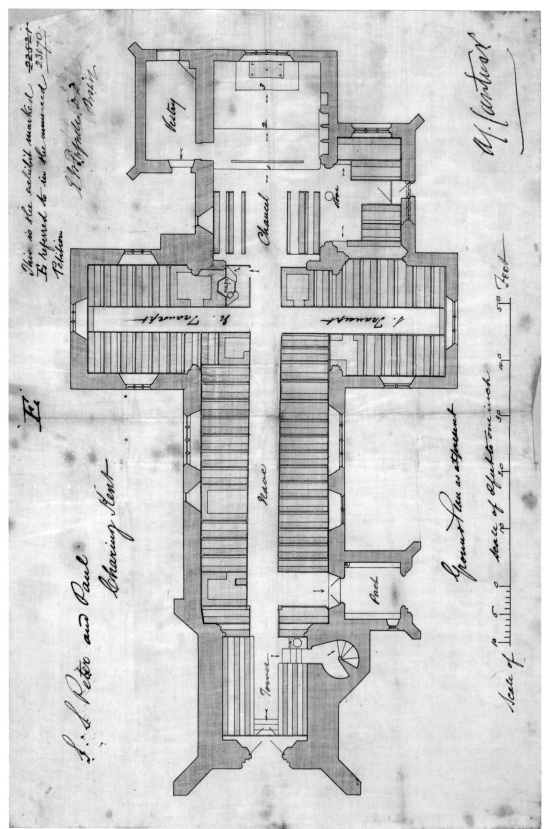

Fig. 5.16 Plan of the church in 1878 before the re-ordering (© Canterbury Cathedral Archives: DCb E/F/Charing/2)

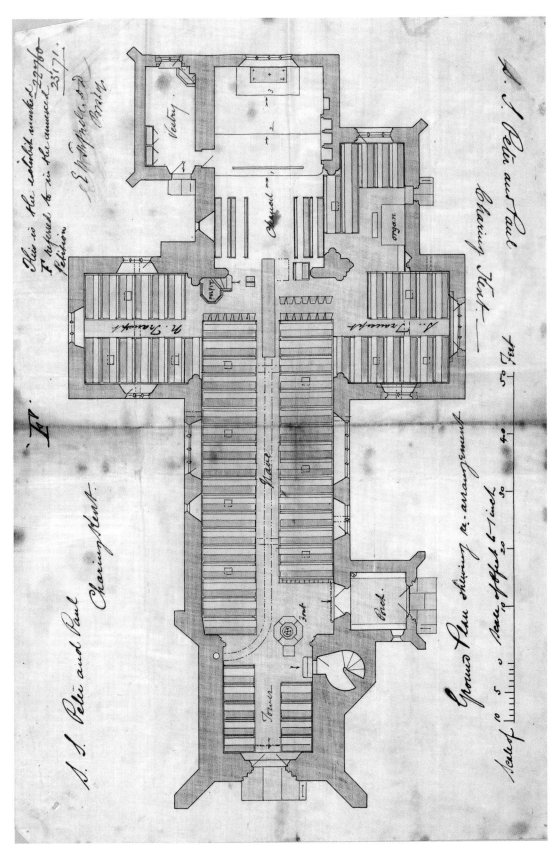

Fig. 5.17 Plan of proposed re-ordering in 1878 (© Canterbury Cathedral Archives: DCb E/F/Charing/2)

Fig. 5.18 Elizabeth Ludwell Monument, 1765 (S Pearson)

The detailed 'before' and 'after' plans annexed to the faculty show a church packed full of seats (Figs 5.16, 5.17). In the first there appears to be a screen or thin wall across the west end with a doorway in it; the west doorway opens over level ground and the steps down into the church only begin beyond this second doorway. The pews appear to be the box pews referred to earlier and they filled the whole of the nave, the north and south transepts and the Lady Chapel. The second plan shows new seating. This is clearly the present day Victorian pitch-pine pews; they filled the whole of the nave and transepts, and extended halfway into the crossing. The west screen was removed and the steps moved so that the door opened over them, as it does today. The font appears to have been raised on a plinth and moved slightly forward of the west arch. The pulpit position, orientation and steps, shown rather differently in the first plan, are drawn exactly as they are today, indicating that this was when the pulpit was lowered and repositioned. Both drawings illustrate the organ in the Lady Chapel, even though the faculty states that the chapel to which the organ was to be moved was on the north side of the church (probably an undetected error in the handwritten document). The peal of six bells was made by John Taylor & Co. of Loughborough and was the gift of Bishop Tufnell who was a major driving force behind the restoration work. His gift is recorded on a brass plaque above the tower door.

Memorials

The church does not have many memorials. There are no early ones, probably because the fact that Charing was an archiepiscopal manor meant there was no dominant wealthy family in the parish. A few late-medieval brasses are suggested by several slabs in the floor, two at the entrance to the chancel, one in the nave aisle and one at the south door entrance, but any evidence of images or inscriptions has completely worn away.

Among the most significant surviving monuments are those in the north transept relating to the Honywood and Sayer families of Pett (Figs 3.9, 3.10). The Lady Chapel is almost completely given over to the Dering family who lived at Peirce House and Wickens in the seventeenth centuries. One of the floor slabs records the death of Catherine Dering who was the daughter of William Levet who attended Charles I on the scaffold at his execution. Several memorials of both the Sayer and the Dering families refer to remains lying nearby, which tends to confirm the existence of vaults under the floor. One of these is under the organ console and it appears to contain four burials. In 1854 John Huckstepp, gent., sought a faculty to build a vault on the south side of the church under certain pews, between the reading desk and the south door. It was intended for his daughter Mary and later for his family and himself. The faculty was granted 'so long as [there is] no damage to the church or the graves therein'. There is no evidence of the completion of this vault but there are graves of earlier Huckstepps in the churchyard.

A memorial at the eastern end of the north wall of the nave is interesting in that it includes part of the will of Elizabeth Ludwell who lived at Ludwell House in the High Street and died at the age of 86 in 1765. Among her bequests were £2,560 to the parish and £500 each to found two exhibitions at Oriel College, Oxford (Fig. 5.18)

Fig. 5.19 The stained glass east window showing the four evangelists (S Pearson)

Stained Glass

The stained glass windows are all nineteenth- or twentieth-century additions or insertions in older windows. The lancet in the nave has two shields inserted in it. The top one was made up in the late 1940s by a stained glass specialist for Dr Littledale, who lived in Wakeley House. Some fragments of medieval glass were claimed to have come from Peirce House but no connection with the Brent family could be established. The origin of the lower shield is not known and it seems likely that Dr Littledale had both shields inserted.

The first lancet in the chancel has stained glass illustrations of the birth, crucifixion and resurrection of Christ and was given in memory of William John Groves 1808-66. The east window is shown in the 1840 drawing with plain diamond lights (Fig. 5.8), but a very dark postcard of *c.*1890 shows the figures inserted in each of the main panels and these are presumably the evangelists as they are today. It is interesting that the names are in German – St Mattheus, St Markus, St Lukas and St Johannes – Dr Sebastian Strobl, head of the glass studio in Canterbury Cathedral, wondered if the window might have been transferred to Charing from another site. Figure 5.19 shows the window as it is today.

The west window, according to the Rev. Fotheringham, was given by friends of Bishop Tufnell and must have been installed about the same time as the restoration of 1878. It commemorates four incidents in the lives of the apostles to whom the church is dedicated. They are: the call of St Peter, the warning of St Peter's death, the conversion of St Paul and the death of St Paul.

The remaining stained glass windows were all given as memorials to relatives and benefactors during the late nineteenth century. They depict biblical scenes.

An afterthought – floor levels

In all the previous studies and essays on the church no mention has been made of the floor level within the church in relation to those outside and yet there is a rather striking difference. Taking three points, the large clear windows in the south and north nave and the window in the east wall of the north transept the difference in height between the ground outside and the level of the floor inside is 45cm (18in), 67cm (26in) and 74cm (29in) respectively. Examination of the piers in the great west arch shows that the finished pedestals start at a height of 69cm (27in) above ground level. The stone work below and all round the base of the tower behind the pews is very rough, suggesting that the foundations have been exposed. This impression is enhanced by the presence of steps up to the tower and the west door. It is as if the floor of the church has been lowered, or the floor of the tower was originally higher. Reference has already been made to the pre-restoration drawing attached to the 1878 faculty (Fig. 5.16) which shows the west door opening over level ground with the steps down commencing only beyond a partition wall. Is it possible that when built in the sixteenth century, the floor of the whole tower was considerably higher than it is today? Even allowing for the accumulation of material around the church over the centuries this difference in levels is puzzling and may bear further investigation.

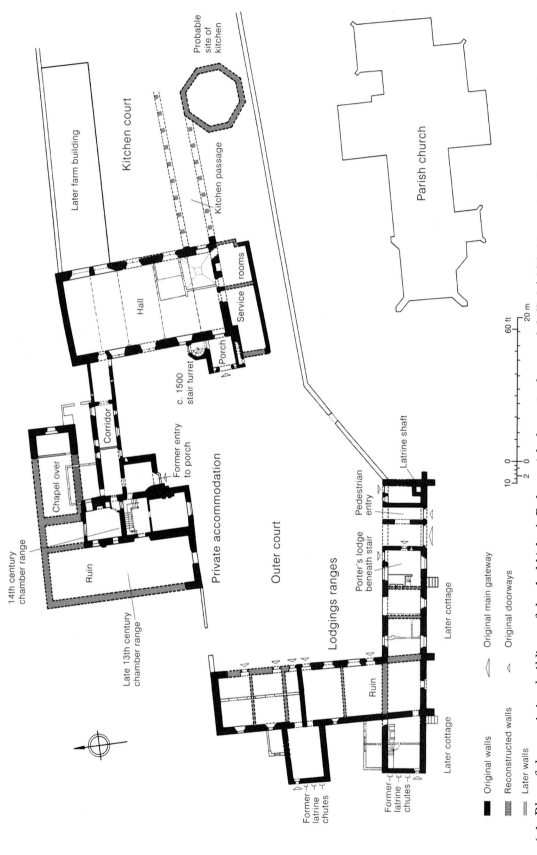

Later farm building

Kitchen court

Probable
site of
kitchen

Kitchen passage

Hall

Service
rooms

Porch

c. 1500
stair turret

Corridor

Former entry
to porch

Chapel over

14th century
chamber range

Ruin

Private accommodation

Late 13th century
chamber range

Outer court

Lodgings ranges

Porter's lodge
beneath stair

Pedestrian
entry

Latrine shaft

Later cottage

Ruin

Later cottage

Former
latrine
chutes

Former
latrine
chutes

Parish church

60 ft

20 m

10

0

2

0

2

■ Original walls

▷ Original main gateway

▨ Reconstructed walls

◁ Original doorways

= Later walls

Fig. 6.1 Plan of the surviving buildings of the Archbishop's Palace with the main features labelled (A T Adams, based upon a survey by the Royal Commission on the Historical Monuments of England, 1996)

Chapter 6: The Archbishop's Palace

by Sarah Pearson

Introduction

The presence of the Archbishop's Palace in the centre of the village distinguishes Charing from surrounding settlements (Fig. 6.1). A large estate, later manor, was given to the church of Canterbury in the eighth century, and remained the property of the archbishops of Canterbury until the Reformation when the manor (it was never called a palace in medieval times) passed into the hands of Henry VIII. There was probably always a dwelling on the site, but nothing is known about it until the late Middle Ages. At that time, the archbishop of Canterbury was the wealthiest landowner in Kent. He had seventeen estates in and around the county, each one within a day's ride of the next; he could travel from Lambeth to Canterbury by way of Croydon, Otford, Maidstone and Charing, spending one or more nights in each place, feeding his large retinue on the local produce and settling business on the surrounding estate. Some of the archbishops' medieval residences have been completely destroyed, but remains of several survive today. Among them Charing is of interest in that its buildings date largely to the early fourteenth century. Most of the other residences were rebuilt during the next two centuries. The late-medieval Charing estate comprised about 300 acres, with 4.94 acres, including the manor house, inside a walled enclosure. The estate remained this size after the Middle Ages, and is illustrated on a map made for the Wheler family in 1736 (Fig. 2.1).

Fig. 6.2 Aerial view of the church and palace, showing the outer court to the left and the remains of the kitchen court behind the church (I Gambrill)

The eleventh and twelfth centuries

Before the Conquest nothing is known about the manor house at Charing, although it was said to be one of the favoured residences of Archbishop Dunstan (959-88). It is likely that the residence was built in timber, and no evidence for stone structures survives until the twelfth century. From the late eleventh century to the early thirteenth, archiepiscopal property was administered by lessees, called 'farmers'. These were important local men who had all the profits from the estates, but in return paid a hefty annual sum (see pp. 9, 11) and were obliged to provide for the archbishop and his household for up to two weeks a year, thus ensuring that the residences could be used as a stopping-off point as the archbishop travelled between his estates. The best known Charing lessee was Adam of Charing, who had property in Canterbury and elsewhere. He inherited the farm of Charing from his father and was lessee in the time of Archbishop Thomas Beckett (1162-70), of whom he was initially a close supporter, although he later fell out with him and was excommunicated by the archbishop when in exile in 1169. After Beckett's death Adam became steward to later archbishops and seems to have died a wealthy man around 1206-7. Beckett was another archbishop who was said to be fond of Charing, and a single, simple late twelfth-century stone capital of so-called 'cushion' form, may date from his time. It has been reused in the wall of the fifteenth-century accommodation block, and its size suggests it came from a small stone building, perhaps the chapel or part of the private ranges.

Fig. 6.3 a) and b) Panorama of the south face of the chamber ranges and west face of the hall and porch (Kent Buildings Preservation Trust)

The great chamber and the chapel

In the late thirteenth century, two documents survive which help us to picture the manor. The first, in the time of Archbishop Kilwardby (1272-1278) is an account of receipts and expenditure for the year 1273/4. Because of repairs that were undertaken, various parts of the dwelling and surrounding buildings were mentioned. A plasterer was paid for daubing the wardrobe in the new chamber (the term wardrobe possibly indicating a room or closet for possessions and/or a latrine), and there was mention of the kitchen, the almonry and the gate. In addition to the domestic and official rooms there was clearly a working farm with a great barn, a hay barn, a vetch barn, cowshed, oxhouse, and a pigsty against the churchyard wall.

A decade later, in 1283-5, Archbishop Pecham (1279-1292) commissioned a survey of his entire manor of Charing, and the services required of some of his tenants tell us of the presence of the private treasury or chamber, the kitchen, bakehouse, brewhouse, gatehouse, piggeries and corn and hay barns. In other words the documents paint a picture of a large and well-equipped dwelling and farm. The main survivor of this period seems to be the flint and stone ruin directly opposite the gate, dated by the roll-moulded profile of its projecting string courses (Fig. 6.3a). Since the range has lost its roof, floors and windows it is impossible to reconstruct its original appearance in detail, but enough survives to show that there was a great chamber on the first floor, heated by a fireplace built into the east wall and lit by a large window in the south gable wall. It was possibly Kilwardby's 'new' chamber. The rest of the private accommodation was rebuilt later.

Remains of the Archiepiscopal Palace at Charing!

*Fig. 6.4 The remains of the east window of the chapel in 1833 (*The Gentleman's Magazine, *vol. 103, pt 2 (1833), plate opp. p. 113)*

The only other building which may be contemporary with the chamber is the fragmentary remains of the first-floor chapel to its north east. Only part of the ground-floor walls beneath the chapel survive today, but it was described by Hasted in 1798 as 'standing entire, being built of squared stone, mixed with flints; on the south side of it are three windows with pointed arches, and at the east end a much larger one of the same form'. The east wall, with the outline of the full-height east window was illustrated in 1833 (Fig. 6.4).

Expansion and new buildings

In 1294 Robert Winchelsea became archbishop of Canterbury (1294-1313), and we know from the registers that, as in the case of Beckett and Dunstan before him, he liked being at Charing. In his earlier years he came two or three times a year, sometimes staying for several days. Almost immediately it appears that he had plans for expanding the manor house, for in May 1298, when he was in Charing for ten days, he sought permission from the king to enlarge the site at the expense of the public road which ran on the south side of his property. Until then the road from Lenham to Ashford seems to have come into Charing along what is now School Road straight across the High Street, into the market place south of the manor and past one or other side of the church. But Winchelsea wished to take in land to the south of his courtyard and move the public highway. His application was granted in June that year, but the document does not make clear where the new road was to run. It is probable, however, that it was then that the dog-leg crossing of the High Street was created and the eastern section of the road to Ashford was moved to run south of the church along the present footpath (Fig. 6.5). This may have remained the main Ashford road for some time since the fifteenth-century houses at the junctions of the High Street and both School

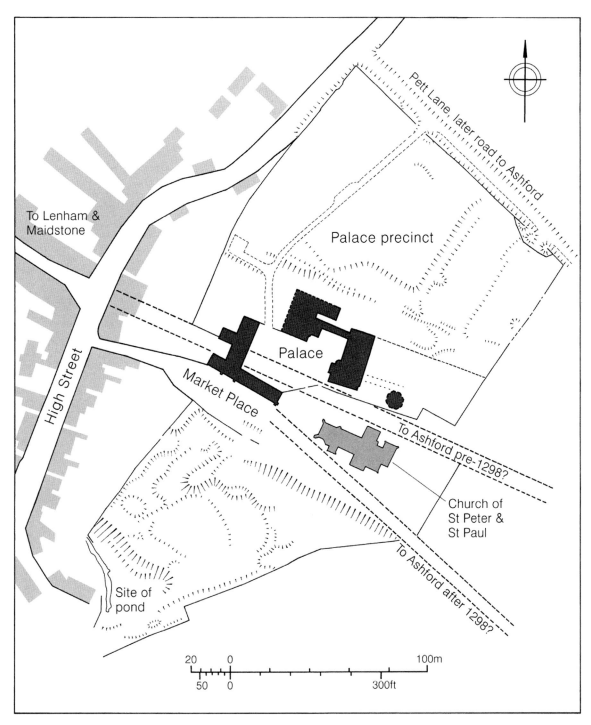

Fig. 6.5 Site plan of the palace and surrounding land, showing the probable line of the roads before and after 1298 (A T Adams, based upon a survey by the Royal Commission on the Historical Monuments of England, 1996)

Fig. 6.6 Sketch of hall, porch and service end (S Dray)

Fig. 6.7 Fourteenth-century hall window and part of porch, with added stair turret of c.1500 (T Reed)

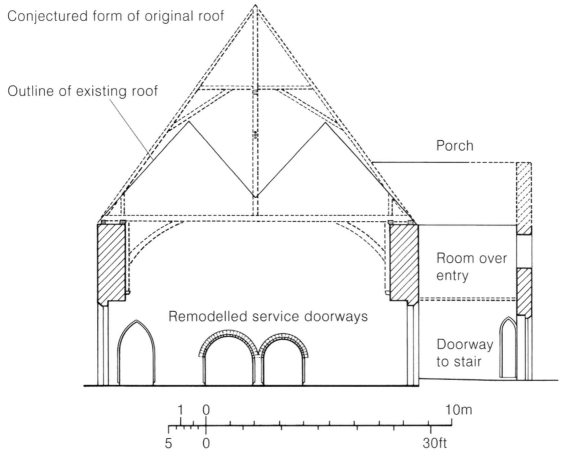

Fig. 6.8 Cross section through the great hall with a reconstruction of the possible form of the original roof (A T Adams, based upon a survey by the Royal Commission on the Historical Monuments of England, 1996)

Road and the Market Place face towards the latter two, implying they were more important than the High Street. Later on the Ashford road was diverted to the north of the archbishop's property, along Pett Lane, where it remained until the eighteenth century.

The enlargement of the archbishop's court allowed a larger hall to be erected as well as the gatehouse range that we see today. This was probably considered essential in order to accommodate a growing retinue. During the early fourteenth century the number of staff travelling with major personages was increasing, and at the top levels of society there was an obligation on wealthy landowners to dispense hospitality on a grand scale since there was nowhere else for the aristocracy to stay when on their travels. In the case of the archbishop this sometimes included putting up royalty. King Edward I stayed in Charing in 1297 and 1299, and one can imagine the archbishop feeling under pressure to upgrade the private accommodation for such occasions, and also to remodel the service and lodging areas that were required to cater for the enlarged household at such times.

The hall

No doubt there had been an earlier hall at Charing, but the present one was a completely new building of the early fourteenth century, almost certainly planned after 1298 (Figs 6.1, 6.3b). Much of this great hall has been destroyed and rebuilt as a barn, but enough original material

Fig. 6.9 The south range and western projections from the Market Place (S Pearson)

remains to establish its main features (Fig. 6.8). It was 10.7m (35ft) wide x 21.8m (71ft 6in) long and was divided into five bays by huge roof trusses spanning the entire width and carried on corbels set half way up the walls – two of them remain either side of the present barn doorways. Each bay was lit by a trefoil headed window surmounted by an octafoil with elongated cusps, one of which survives on the west side (Fig. 6.7). The two-storey porch on the west wall contained the main entrance into the hall through a now-blocked doorway. The ground floor of the porch remains from this time, although the upper storey was partly rebuilt later in the Middle Ages (Figs 6.6, 6.7). At the north end of the hall there would have been a raised dais for the archbishop and his guests, who entered the hall from the private chambers by a doorway (now blocked) on the west wall. At the south end of the hall two central doorways (also blocked) almost certainly opened into a buttery and a pantry (the service rooms where wet and dry stores were kept). The rough outlines of the doorways are visible in the wall although the original surrounds have gone, and the service end beyond them has been completely rebuilt.

Because the church and churchyard lay so close to the south end of the hall, there was no room for the normal arrangement found in most great halls in which a detached kitchen lay beyond the service end (Fig. 6.1). Instead, it was sited in a courtyard to the east of the hall, reached by a doorway in the east wall of the hall directly opposite the main entrance (Fig. 6.2). The east courtyard is now a farmyard with no visible early remains, but in 1833 it was reported that a building of octagonal form with 'sewers' and a floor of tiles set on edge had been uncovered in this area, and it was suggested that this was the kitchen floor. The suggestion makes sense, as the position is likely to be correct and the kitchens of great houses in the fourteenth-century were often polygonal. Documentary reference to a 'tresaunce' suggests a covered passage between the hall and the kitchen, possibly of two-storeys as has been found elsewhere. Other service buildings, such as the bakery and the brewhouse, were probably located around the kitchen courtyard. It is hoped that one day archaeology will reveal more about this part of the site.

The size and details of the great hall can be compared with those of several large halls in Kent and Sussex. Penshurst Place, Ightham Mote, Battel Hall at Leeds in Kent, and Mayfield in Sussex, another manor owned by the archbishop, all had large and imposing arch-braced roof trusses; but most of these were built between 1330 and 1350, a considerable time after Archbishop Winchelsea is likely to have erected his hall at Charing. It has therefore been reconstructed in Figure 6.8 with the kind of roof more commonly found in the years between 1280 and 1320. These were less visually eye-catching, of plainer construction, with simple braces to the collars and often with a central post (called a king-strut) from tiebeam to apex. Examples remain at The Table Hall, Canterbury (probably before 1285), The Deanery, Chartham (1303) and

Fig. 6.10 The porter's doorway and window under the entrance archway (S Pearson)

Fig. 6.11 The inner face of the gateway, and blocked doorways to a chamber and a large staircase in the south range (S Pearson)

Court Lodge, Great Chart (1313), all built by Christ Church Priory, Canterbury, and the roofs of the Guest Hall, Canterbury, and the great chamber at Samlestone Grange, Margate, both constructed in the late thirteenth century by St Augustine's Abbey, Canterbury. The Charing hall roof is likely to have been more like these, although the fact that there were timber wall posts carried on corbels looks forward to the next generation of more elaborate roofs erected in the second quarter of the fourteenth century.

The gatehouse range

Once Archbishop Winchelsea had gained extra space on the south side of the main or outer court he expanded the accommodation and built the surviving south range and west ranges (Figs 6.1, 6.9). The large gateway towards the east end of the south range, formerly closed by a portcullis, was for carts and horses to enter the courtyard, and had a small pedestrian gate to its east. The porter's room lay to the west where there is a small blocked doorway and a blocked window which would have allowed him to monitor what was going on (Fig. 6.10). Much of the rest of the range has been destroyed or rebuilt, but enough clues remain to indicate its original layout. At ground-floor level a number of blocked doorways survive on the north and east sides (Fig. 6.11). They show that there was a small room to the east of the gateway, and others to the west. The first of the western doorways was larger than the others and almost certainly opened onto a grand stair which would appear to have been the only access to the first floor at that time. Smaller blocked doorways further round the courtyard opened into ground-floor rooms. In the early fourteenth century it was normal for ground-floor rooms to be entered directly from outside and for the stairs to the upper floor to be reached from an external doorway.

Fig. 6.12 First-floor fireplace above the gateway in the south range (S Pearson)

At the top of the stairs there was a large chamber at the east end heated by a fireplace in the north wall: the corbels to carry its lintel and the herringbone brickwork at its back can still be seen above the gateway (Fig. 6.12). This large chamber also had a private latrine chute, so it must have been reserved for someone of importance. Not much detail of the rest of the first floor survives, but it is likely that a series of chambers opened round the courtyard, each opening from the next and none of them heated – internal corridors and heated chambers were later developments. They were almost certainly lodging chambers, really dormitories, for the retinues of officials and servants who accompanied the archbishop and his guests. Two large wings projecting to the west (one now a cottage, the other a stable) served as latrine blocks containing communal latrines for the lodgings. The proof lies in six small ground-floor arches, three in each of the west walls of the projecting wings, which were for clearing out the refuse (Fig. 6.13). In addition a knee-high shallow shelf is visible on the first-floor west wall of the northern block, and this seems to have been where the wooden seating was fixed. This is a rare survival, for by the late fourteenth century communal toilet blocks were being replaced by individual latrines to each chamber. Charing is unusual in preserving evidence for an arrangement that very soon became old-fashioned.

Fig. 6.13 Blocked arches for clearing out latrines (S Pearson)

The archbishop entertains

In March 1348 an expense account survives which itemises the expenditure required to accommodate Archbishop Stratford (1343-1348) for two nights at Charing, on one of which he entertained the abbot of Faversham. The accounts only deal with additional expenses, so the wages of the permanent staff travelling with the archbishop were not included. Nonetheless, the number of people catered for and the amount of food and drink needed are staggering. Hay was required for eighty horses: ten hacks for the archbishop and his household, twelve yearlings, and a large number of pack horses. Wages, expenses and tips

Fig. 6.14 Fourteenth-century chamber range, porch bay and corridor to the hall, all heightened and altered c.1500 and later (S Pearson)

were paid to a baker and two boys helping him, four chapel servants, four valets, fifteen pages, and fifty-eight other boys. Since it was Lent fish was the main item on the menu, and payment was made for 600 herrings, some salted salmon, a sturgeon, and lots of cod, pike, eel, bream, trout and other fish. Over the two nights (separated by a few days in Canterbury) 428 loaves of bread were baked, and 160 gallons of beer and fifteen gallons of wine were required. One can only imagine how much more lavish entertaining the king would have been. The quantity of people and supplies needed for even a short visit like this indicates why the enlarged hall, new lodging ranges, and other buildings which have no doubt gone, were necessary. One may also surmise that the archbishop's visits were well-received in Charing since they brought employment for locals and probably perks for them and their families in the form of extra food and drink.

Additions and rebuilding during the fourteenth and fifteenth centuries

It is likely that the private accommodation was upgraded during the early fourteenth century, and the underlying structure of the eastern range may date from this period, although much altered later. By the 1390s the archbishops needed to be in London near the Court most of the time, and the properties furthest from London became underused and were leased again. However, the archbishop retained the right to reside in Charing as he still needed to travel to Canterbury on occasion.

On the north side of the outer courtyard, the range parallel and to the east of the thirteenth-century chamber block was added or rebuilt in stone and flint during the fourteenth century (Figs 6.3a, 6.14), and today it is difficult to understand exactly how the parts fitted together and functioned. To start with it was of two storeys only and entered by a doorway in its north wall (Fig. 6.1). Probably there was always a range to its east, but whatever was there was remodelled in *c.*1500 when the square block in the angle between the eastern chamber range and the corridor to the hall was turned into a porch-cum-stair turret.

Archbishop Morton (1486-1500) was associated with alterations at Charing. In 1493 he was granted a licence to impress (force into service) stone-cutters and bricklayers to work on his manors in Kent and Sussex, and in the 1530s the antiquary John Leland described him as 'making great building at Charing'. The top storey of the private ranges, with diamond patterns of black headers in red brickwork, is likely to date from this period, providing a large new, heated apartment on the top floor. It was heated by a large but curiously simple fireplace for a room which might have been used to accommodate royalty (Fig. 6.15), but presumably if the king came he may have been lodged in a grand chamber on the first floor. Both upper storeys were accessed by a timber newel (turning) stair in the square bay in the angle between the chamber range and the corridor; this only survives on the upper floors and can now only be reached by putting a ladder up to the external doorway at first-floor height (Fig. 6.14). On the ground floor the square bay was also a porch, with doorways visible internally on both its south and north faces. The outer doorway has been turned into a bay window; the inner one, which opened onto the corridor to the hall, has been blocked. The corridor itself was also rebuilt. Some sort of corridor, originally no doubt of timber, had probably been here a long time, since it is unlikely that the archbishops would ever have got wet when going to dinner in the hall. But it was first remade in flint, and then heightened and altered in brick in *c*.1500. At the same time the porch to the great hall was heightened and a brick stair turret was added on its north side (Fig. 6.7).

After a long period (mid fourteenth to late fifteenth century) during which we have no information, documents show that royalty continued to stay at Charing on occasion. Henry

Fig. 6.15 Fireplace in the second storey of the chamber range, added c.1500 (S Pearson)

VII is known to have come at least twice before Morton's death, and his visits continued during the time of Archbishop Warham (1503-1532). Henry VIII followed in his father's footsteps, coming to Charing on several occasions, and sometimes staying for a week or more. In 1520 he is known to have stopped at Charing on his way to France to meet King Francis I for the Field of the Cloth of Gold, and he also came in the early 1540s, just before he decided to include Charing among the properties which he forced Archbishop Cranmer to concede to him in 1545, thus severing its long connection with the archbishopric of Canterbury. The oddity is that the amount of surviving new accommodation provided is not great, and hardly seems appropriate or lavish enough for the entertainment of royalty. If one compares Charing with the huge brick palace that Archbishop Warham built at Otford in north-west Kent it is very much the poor country cousin. It is possible, therefore, that other new ranges, perhaps built of timber, have vanished without obvious trace. It is not clear that Henry VIII ever came to stay in Charing again after he acquired it in 1545.

The sixteenth century and later

Throughout the sixteenth century the buildings and surrounding enclosure were leased to local gentry. The leases stipulated only that the archbishop retained the right to the great stable and a barn for hay although, as discussed above, both the archbishop and the king stayed on more than one occasion prior to 1545. Several of the lessees were members of the Brent family. John Brent took a lease from the archbishop in 1528, followed by another in 1541. On his death the lease passed to his son, and subsequently to another Brent, of Willesborough near Ashford. Several other leases to gentry followed. In 1575 one William Lovelace was accused of burning, selling and spoiling the old hall and other buildings and taking away 'iron, glass, lead, wainscot, brick and tile', although in the end not a great deal of damage could be proved. A stone plaque with the date 1586 over what was then the porch doorway to the private accommodation (now the bay window) may relate to one of the lessees, but it could have been inserted at any time and does not prove that building work took place at that date.

In 1593 Nicholas Gilborne was granted a lease. He was not a local man, but was later knighted, and in 1611-12 became High Sheriff of Kent, using Charing as his official residence. In 1629, under Charles I, the crown sold the house and manor. Sir Nicholas or his immediate heirs were not in a position to buy it, although the family remained as tenants. The first new owners were not local, but in 1635 it was bought by Sir Robert Honywood the elder of Pett. In the later seventeenth century it passed to Robert, the eldest son of Sir Robert Honywood the younger, while his father was still alive. After Robert was attainted (p.25) it was administered with the rest of the estate for the benefit of his widow and sons, and passed after his death to his eldest son, Walter, who died in 1686. The younger son also having died, the manor passed to a cousin, another Robert, who in 1692 sold it for £1,430 to Sir George Wheler, great grandson of Sir Nicholas Gilborne.

The Wheler family had been royalist in sympathy and George was born in exile on the continent in 1651. But they returned to Charing at the Restoration and, according to George's memoirs, his father Charles (son of Gilborne's daughter who had married a Wheler) first completed a lease on the palace, and then moved to Park House, Little Chart which belonged to the Darells. George (knighted 1682) had warm memories of the palace as a child, reporting that it was 'a noble house, planted with orchard walls of the best fruit, fine gardens, rare trees and plants', and that there was an excellent library. Thus in 1692 he took the opportunity to purchase the manor and manor house from the Honywoods. His main estates, however, were in Hampshire and Wiltshire and he probably never lived in Charing as an adult. When he made his will in 1719 he left the palace (possibly the first time the title of palace was used) to his three youngest daughters whilst they remained unmarried. On their marriages or deaths it was to pass to his younger son, Granville. By the time of Sir George's death in 1724 he had added a number of other local manors to his estates, including Otterden and Stalisfield, and Granville and his heirs resided at Otterden Place. Charing remained in possession of the Wheler family for well over two hundred years, the house and demesne farm mostly being leased. They were sold to the Homewood family in the twentieth century, although the lordship of the manor of Charing remained with the Whelers until the death of the last Granville Wheler in 2004.

In the seventeenth century, the private apartments became the farmhouse with the other ranges round the two courtyards turned to farm buildings. We do not know where the earlier agricultural buildings had been located, but the fact that half of Clewards, the green in front of the palace, was called Old Barn Yard in the key to the 1736 Wheler estate map (Fig. 2.2; plot D, coloured red, to the south of the church), may indicate that this was where they had originally been situated. Once the main house had become a farm various alterations took place within the courtyards. The rear of the private apartments was largely rebuilt in brick, the stone corridor linking the house to the old hall was heightened, and parts of the gatehouse range were turned to cottages for farm workers. The great hall became a barn and its roof was rebuilt with the original single span remade as two lower spans supported by central posts (Fig. 6.8); an oast house was inserted in one corner. The ranges round the kitchen courtyard were also demolished or rebuilt as farm buildings. In most cases the structures were not totally replaced because they could be turned to new uses with relatively little outlay. As a result Charing is among the most complete of the archbishops' fourteenth-century residences in England, and of considerable importance for the light it sheds on the kind of accommodation required in a high-status dwelling of the early fourteenth century.

Fig. 7.1 Vicarage Cottage, a Wealden house with a recessed open hall, refronted in 1885 (S Pearson)

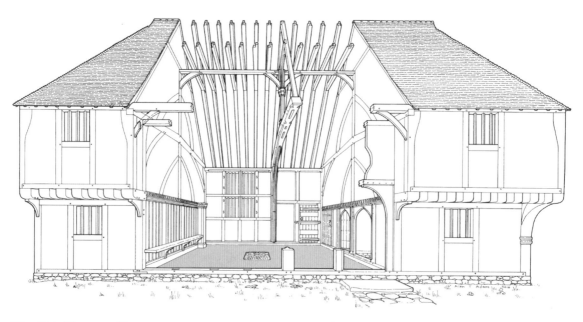

Fig. 7.2 Vicarage Cottage reconstructed as built c.1400 (A T Adams)

Chapter 7: Historic Houses of Charing

by Sarah Pearson

Introduction

Charing parish includes a village (called a town in earlier years), surrounded by a large rural area. The earliest houses were erected 500-600 years ago, and over forty were built in the sixteenth century or before. Not unnaturally they have all been refurbished or expanded in later years, work which often conceals the early core from the outside. Many more good buildings were erected from scratch in the seventeenth, eighteenth and nineteenth centuries, and these have been less altered. Such a large number of surviving historic buildings is not unusual for this part of Kent, which has almost always been one of the wealthiest regions of England. Not every historic house in Charing can be mentioned in this essay, which seeks to provide a general overview and discuss the more important or better preserved examples remaining from each period.

The Middle Ages (*c.*1300-*c.*1520)

Across Kent a few timber-framed houses of manorial status survive which are 700 years old, but none have so far been found in this parish. The first timber-framed buildings to remain were built about 1400, after the horrors of the Black Death had killed between one third and one half of the population. People who survived often prospered since land was plentiful and labour scarce and therefore well-paid. Thus in the late fourteenth and early fifteenth centuries new, durable houses began to be built in some numbers. Among them are three in or near Charing 'town'.

The earliest may be Vicarage Cottage (Map 2.3). It has changed a lot over the years, and the exterior is now as seen in Figure 7.1. Inside, a well-built, timber-framed medieval house of four structural bays remains (Fig. 7.2). The two central bays formed the hall, originally open to the roof, and at each end there were extra bays of two storeys, i.e. with chambers above the ground-floor rooms. The end bays were jettied, that is to say the first floors projected to the south front, and the upper floor of the east bay also projected at the east end. The reconstruction illustrates some features which can no longer be seen, but can be postulated from similar houses. The hall was entered by a doorway in the position of the present front door, with another doorway opposite in the back wall. It would have been lit by large windows on both front and back walls, much as the front is lit today. These would not have been glazed, but closed only by shutters: windows each side were essential so that the prevailing weather could be shut out when necessary. The hall would have been heated by an open hearth, which was probably built on a base made of bricks set on edge, and from this the smoke would have curled up to the roof timbers above. At its centre the roof was spanned by an open truss with large braces rising to a tiebeam that supported a crown post with a decorated cap and base. Although the evidence in this house has been obscured, the drawing shows a fitted bench at the left-hand or parlour end of the hall with a decorated beam, called a dais beam, above it; this was common in most smart open-hall houses in Kent, marking the seat of honour for the head of the household and his family. A doorway to the parlour and the stair to the chamber above it lay at the rear next to the back wall, hidden here by a small screen protecting the bench from draughts. At the right-hand or service end of the hall, two doorways opened into two service rooms with a third doorway at the back for a second set of stairs to the chamber above that end. In this particular house there was also a second decorated beam, something that is not very common and reserved for the best-quality houses. The service rooms, found in hundreds of Kent's medieval houses, are commonly called the pantry, for storing bread and dry goods, and the buttery for beer or wet goods, although in practice they could be used for all kinds of purposes. While much of this drawing is reconstruction, the arrangement of medieval houses was so standardised in Kent that we can be fairly sure that this was how the rooms and decorative details were arranged.

Because the upper rooms at the ends projected at the front, the hall appears to be recessed, although, if one looks at the footprint on the ground one can see that it was not. The effect is accentuated by the fact that the house is surmounted by a single east-west roof, probably always covered in peg-tiles, which spanned the whole building, the rafters across the hall being supported by a 'flying' plate, i.e. one that lay in line with the jettied end bays and therefore some way in front of the hall wall, as is still the case for part of the roof today. This distinctive arrangement of the roof over the hall and ends is so common in rural Kent and east Sussex, that such houses are known as 'Wealdens'. Details of the timber mouldings and joints, including the pointed form of the door heads, suggest Vicarage Cottage was built between about 1380 and 1420. Together with a later range at right-angles, it became the vicarage and may always have been so, although its early history is unknown.

Two other houses in Charing town may in part date from much the same time: the rear part of 47 High Street (Wady and Brett's, Map 2.37) and 33 High Street (Peirce House,

Fig. 7.3 Historic houses in Charing High Street (S Pearson)

Map 2.36), which stands back from the road. Most of Peirce House has been rebuilt or demolished, but behind the gabled front wings it still retains one half of an early open hall. In common with medieval buildings everywhere, many houses in Charing were built in phases, and frequently the earliest part to survive has clear signs that it was an addition to a yet earlier building that was itself later rebuilt. This is true of both these examples; in other words there were earlier houses on their sites, probably built during the fourteenth century, or perhaps even earlier.

As discussed in Chapter 2, the market place, first mentioned in 1285, lay in front of the archbishop's manor house. Stalls and shops continued to be documented there until at least 1500, but by the fifteenth century, the High Street was lined with well-built timber houses, many of which probably contained shops. Gradually this became the main trading area of the town and the market ceased to function, even though its name has been retained to this day.

So much refronting and rebuilding of the High Street houses has taken place over the

Fig. 7.4 Brocton, Charing Heath. The parlour end of the former open hall with the doorway to the stair, medieval panelling, a decorative dais beam and evidence for a short projecting screen (S Pearson)

years that it is difficult to identify some of the medieval houses from the outside (Fig. 7.3). But examination of the interiors reveals their large joists, early windows or doorways, and in particular the roof timbers above. In the Middle Ages open halls and first-floor rooms were open to the roofs. These were only hidden by inserted ceilings in the seventeenth and eighteenth centuries, thereby becoming inaccessible until they were opened up when first water tanks, and later insulation, were introduced. Constructed of oak, the roofs are usually in good repair, particularly where the timbers have been pickled by smoke from the open hearth, so that today they allow us to identify the medieval buildings. From smoke-blackening, surviving decorated crown posts and early partitions in the roof, one can learn a great deal about how the rooms below were arranged. In Charing town no less than fourteen fifteenth-century or earlier houses remain, to which may be added at least fifteen more in the rural part of the parish. Of course this is not the total number of houses that existed, but it has been estimated that they formed the dwellings of around twenty per cent of the households recorded in the parish in 1557, by which time the medieval population had increased considerably.

In the rural areas there were several large Wealden houses, not dissimilar to Vicarage Cottage, with two-bay open halls and jettied ends projecting at the front making the open halls appear recessed: Barnfield (Fig. 3.2), Brockton and Sandpett are surviving examples.

Although later refaced in brick, many fine internal details survive at Brockton, including medieval panelling and a decorated dais beam behind and above the site of the dais bench at the parlour end of the hall (Fig. 7.4). The post beside the doorway has a mortice indicating the former presence of a short screen shielding the bench from the doorway, as shown in the reconstruction of Vicarage Cottage (Fig. 7.2). Other large houses, such as Swan Street Farm and Newlands Manor (probably the farmhouse rather than the manor house itself), had the same plan but the multi-storeyed bays were jettied only to the ends, so that the long façade was flat-fronted (Fig. 7.5). At Pett Place and Raywood Farm, the medieval buildings have been too altered for their original form to be easily identifiable, although we know they contained open halls. Hunger Hatch Cottage, a small farmhouse on the southern edge of the parish, is an unusual survival which had not only an open hall but open ends as well and thus no upstairs chambers at all to start with.

In Charing town some of the houses were free-standing properties, with a similar amount of accommodation to that in Vicarage Cottage. This included The Moat (Map 2.16), an isolated house which was Charing's rectory or parsonage house. Built in the late fifteenth century it is one of the largest Wealden hall houses in Kent. Some of the High Street houses were likewise freestanding, with small passageways at each side leading to the rear. The largest is Nos. 44, 46 and 48 (Fig. 7.6, Map 2.11), and the wide timber joists of the end bay in No. 48 can still be seen in the Post Office. Other whole or part Wealden houses occur at 52, 54 High Street (Hogben's butcher's shop and house; Fig. 3.4, Map 2.9), the front bays of 47 High Street (Wady and Brett's; Map 2.37)), which faced School Road, 26 High Street (Ridgemount; Fig. 7.18, Map 2.15), and the core of 58, 60, 62 High Street (Elizabethan Court, formerly The Swan Inn; Fig. 7.19, Map 2.8).

Fig. 7.5 Swan Street Farmhouse, Charing Heath Road. A former open-hall house with a jetty to the left end only (S Pearson)

Fig. 7.6 44, 46, 48 High Street. The middle section was formerly an open hall (S Pearson)

Fig. 7.7 30, 32 High Street. Two small medieval houses. No. 32 (left) formerly had a tiny open hall (S Pearson)

Fig. 7.8 32 High Street. Crown-post roof heavily sooted from the former open fire (S Pearson)

Fig. 7.9 Crown-post roof over the cross wing of 19 High Street (S Pearson)

Most of these houses have only single-bay open halls, and therefore do not have the free-standing central crown posts which only occur in larger houses with two-bay halls. Often their two-storeyed end bays have been reconstructed and it is not possible to be certain whether there were extra bays at both ends of the hall, or only at one. The latter arrangement certainly occurred at 30 and 32 High Street (Fig. 7.7, Map 2.12 & 13), now concealed behind Georgian frontages. No. 32 was only 7m (23ft) in length, containing a tiny open hall 2.7m (9ft) long, its roof heavily sooted by smoke from an open hearth below (Fig. 7.8), and an end bay to the north with a chamber on the first floor. This type of house is well-known in towns across England and is thought to have been home to small craftsmen or wage-earners. No. 30 High Street is slightly larger and may always have had an enclosed fireplace heating the hall, probably with a first floor above; thus, despite having a medieval crown-post roof it may date to the early years of the sixteenth century.

Several houses in the High Street probably had shops at the front of the two-storeyed ends. This can only be proved at 19 High Street (Fig. 7.10, Map 2.33), where a small cross wing at right angles to the street was attached at its south side to a hall that was later rebuilt. The wing had a single large chamber on the first floor spanned by a central free-standing crown-post in the roof which would originally have been visible from the chamber below (Fig. 7.9).

On the ground floor two doorways entered the wing from the original hall. At the front was a shop, as shown by framing for a large shop window surviving on the street frontage and visible inside. Behind the shop a central beam with mortices beneath it for studs indicates the site of a partition between two rooms, and in the centre of the beam further mortices reveal that there was a small internal window, which would have allowed the occupant of the rear room to see into the shop at the front. Evidence on the ceiling joists and a surviving doorway suggest that 48 High Street was also divided into two, almost certainly with a shop at the front, although in that case there is no surviving evidence for the shop window. Probably the majority of the High Street houses incorporated shops, but rebuilding of most of the front walls has destroyed the evidence.

Thanks to surviving early documents, there is one fifteenth-century house in Charing whose interior can be described in more detail. This is 33 High Street (Peirce House; Map 2.36), where part of the hall and the kitchen range belonged to the early building mentioned above. Standing back from the street, it was not a standard High Street house, but a large and superior dwelling with its own farm. By the mid fifteenth century the property was owned by the wealthy Brent family. In 1496 when William Brent, lawyer, died, his will indicates that he held extensive lands in Charing and elsewhere, and his probate inventory lists his goods in the various rooms of the house. The hall, hung with fine red woollen hangings, was probably still open to the roof; it was furnished with a cupboard, tables and benches. To the north, now demolished, there was a heated parlour which was still something of a rarity at that

Fig. 7.10 19 High Street. Former open-hall house. The hall, to the left, was rebuilt in the sixteenth century and only a medieval cross wing remains to the right; this contained a shop at the front (S Pearson)

Fig. 7.11 9 High Street (Armada House). An early sixteenth-century house of two storeys with a timber and plaster chimney surviving in the roof (S Pearson)

time. It had green wall hangings, a folding table, a chair, stools, cushions and a 'grett glass', i.e. a mirror, which, like the cushions, was an indication of wealth and high status. The south end of the house, which was shortly to be rebuilt, contained a buttery and a pantry where the household goods and utensils were kept. At the back was a detached range which housed the kitchen where the cooking took place. Upstairs there were at least four bedchambers with bedsteads and fine hangings. Outside in the courtyard a stable contained fifteen horses; and there was a granary full of grain and a barn. Brent owned nearly fifty cattle, including eight oxen for ploughing, and over 130 sheep. This, of course, was not a typical home, but it gives some idea of how the wealthiest members of the parish lived.

The sixteenth century (*c*.1520-*c*.1600)

During the first half of the sixteenth century open halls went out of fashion and hearths were enclosed. Some of the earliest stacks were built of timber and plaster, which was fireproof provided the plastering was well maintained. Sometimes they were inserted into halls which remained open, but often they accompanied the flooring over of an open hall, or were integral to new, fully two-storeyed houses. Such chimney stacks could be replaced very easily without leaving any trace, and most of them were rebuilt in brick in the late sixteenth and seventeenth

Fig. 7.12 27, 29 High Street (Sherborne House), as seen today, and with the shop windows and doorway at the left-hand end reconstructed in the inset to the left (A T Adams)

Fig. 7.13 33 High Street (Peirce House). The early sixteenth-century porch-cum-stair wing with the service wing to the left (S Pearson)

centuries. In a few cases, however, the flue survives at roof level. This is the case at 9 High Street (Armada House; Map 2.31) where two sides of the flue, smoke-blackened on their inner faces, remain next to the later brick stack. Seen from the front of the house (Fig.7.11), the smoke bay is behind the present chimney stack to the left of the central doorway, and would have heated the hall to its left. The front doorway originally opened into a passage crossing the house behind the fireplace, and there were one or two rooms to the right. It is possible that the off-centre bracing on the first floor and lack of a cross rail on the ground floor wall at the right-hand end of the house indicates that the house was a dwelling with a shop, entered by a separate doorway, to the right.

This house and others built during the sixteenth century had jetties right across the front. Another good example is 27, 29 High Street (Sherborne House; Fig. 7.12, Map 2.35). At the south end of the building were two large, unglazed shop windows and a doorway to a passage across the building (see inset to Fig. 7.12). The building may have been a little longer to the south, and certainly had an extra bay to the north. Evidence for internal partitions reveals that both the ground and first floors were originally divided into six or seven small units. It is a puzzling building with a number of unresolved problems, such as how the upper floor was reached. Nonetheless, it is probably safe to say that it was unheated to start with and therefore not a house; it perhaps contained a series of shops or workshops and storage spaces.

The finest example of early sixteenth-century construction in Charing is the remodelling of Peirce House, 33 High Street after William Brent's death in 1495 (Fig. 7.13, Map 2.36). Before his second wife Amy died in 1516, it seems that the south end of the house was entirely rebuilt. Possibly the alteration had been planned in William's lifetime, for it was unusual for a widow to undertake such a major reconstruction. The date is deduced from the main doorway which has two badges in the spandrels, one bearing the impaled arms of Brent and Rosmodres (her family), the impaling indicating that Amy was a widow. The second, a badge of crossed staples denotes the Bergavenny family, to which William and Amy's son John and daughter Margaret were both related by marriage. The new building consisted of a large porch-cum-stair, with a chamber over the porch and small attic above, and a new, probably enlarged, service wing of two rooms with two chambers above. The status of the addition is shown by the close-studded framing on the front, and the moulded joists, decorated doorways (Fig. 7.14), painting and panelling of the interior. Traces of small external doorways in the upper chambers imply that each chamber had a private closet or latrine projecting to the south. Photographs taken in the mid twentieth century, before the demolition of the north end of the house, indicate that the hall and northern rooms were upgraded at the same time.

Another early sixteenth-century structure in the town is a three-bay, two-storey building next to the church and at right angles to Vicarage Cottage, the two ranges now forming a single property and touching at the corners. It later became the main part of the vicarage, and is now known as The Old Vicarage (Map 2.4) but a total lack of evidence for original internal partitions on either floor suggests it began life as a public building such as a church house or hall. The ground floor may have been used only for storage, but the upper floor, which is larger since it was jettied on three sides, formed an unheated room of some grandeur, spanned by two decorative crown-post trusses supported on colonettes with carved capitals. The size of the room, its decoration and the lack of heating, combine to make it likely that the building served a communal rather than domestic function. In 1596 the churchwardens' accounts note a payment for thatching the 'church house', although it is not certain that it refers to this building.

Fig. 7.14 33 High Street (Peirce House). Early sixteenth-century service doorways (S Pearson)

Fig. 7.15 Wickens. The decorative east front of the late sixteenth century (J Grebby)

During the sixteenth century high quality work also took place on some of the outlying properties in the parish. To the east of the town, a new front range was built at Pett Place, whose moulded joists remain in the front hall. The renovation was probably undertaken by the Honywood family who inherited the house by marriage in the mid sixteenth century. Later in the century another fine house was built by the Brents or the Derings at Wickens (Fig. 7.15), to the south-east of Charing. Here decorative external framing and high-quality plaster overmantels to the fireplace surrounds (Fig. 7.16) indicate a minor gentry house of the years around 1600. Smaller houses built during the sixteenth century include Little Swan Street Farmhouse, Charing Heath Road (see below) and Forge Cottage, Charing Heath.

The seventeenth century

One of the earliest seventeenth-century houses in Charing is the front part of The Old House, Station Road (Fig. 7.17, Map 2.22), which was the partial rebuilding of a medieval dwelling that still has fragmentary remains at the back. The new addition was of three storeys with an attic at roof level. A large brick chimney was erected between the two builds to heat a fine room in front with a first-floor chamber lit by a projecting bay window and small frieze windows to either side extending round the corners; such emphasis on fenestration was typical of late sixteenth- and early seventeenth-century houses. In the rural part of the parish several timber-framed houses have thin timbers in their walls and ceilings signifying dates in the seventeenth century rather than earlier. Examples are Hunger Hatch Farmhouse, south of Newlands, and Church Hill Cottage and Thatched Cottage, Church Hill along one side of Charing heath.

Fig. 7.16 Wickens. A chamber fireplace with plaster overmantel (S Pearson)

Fig. 7.17 The Old House, Station Road (S Pearson)

In Charing town, most of the seventeenth-century work consisted of updating earlier houses by addition or replacement. By this time all the open halls had been ceiled over to create chambers on the first floor, and brick chimneys were replacing the timber and plaster flues which had been built during the early sixteenth century. This was when a brick chimney replaced the old timber and plaster flue of 9 High Street blocking the cross passage so that a second fireplace could be added to heat the northern room. At 28 High Street (Hope Haven; Fig. 7.18, Map 2.14) a new cross wing of two storeys and an attic replaced the medieval parlour end of 26 High Street (Ridgemount).

In some cases the walls of earlier buildings needed to be repaired, and this was often done in brick, possibly supplied by the local brickworks at Tile Hill in Charing Heath. Notable external brickwork, including mullioned and transomed windows, can be seen at 58, 60, 62 High Street (Elizabethan Court; Fig. 7.19, Map 2.8), a medieval timber building which had been enlarged and become The Swan Inn by the seventeenth century. Similar brickwork forms the truncated north end of 27, 29 High Street, and in the countryside the service end of Brockton. During the seventeenth and eighteenth centuries, the external walls of many timber-framed houses, such as Barnfield (Fig. 3.2) and Swan Street Farmhouse (Fig. 7.5), were clad in brick with tile hanging above to protect the timbers from the weather.

The hearth tax of 1664

Fireplaces were important new features of many homes, and seventeenth-century probate inventories, although not wholly reliable, can be used as a rough guide to their increased popularity. Before 1625, inventories seldom listed more than one fireplace. By the end of the century nearly half had three or more, with at least one on the first floor.

Whereas the old timber and plaster flues, such as the one at 9 High Street, could serve only a single fireplace, the new brick chimney stacks could have a fireplace on each side and on each floor of the house.

Between 1662 and 1689 a national hearth tax was levied twice a year on the fireplaces of all householders except those who were deemed too poor to pay. Many of the returns were destroyed, but that for the county of Kent survives for Lady Day (25 March) 1664. In Charing parish it shows that Sir Robert Honywood had twenty hearths at Pett Place, which still has some seventeenth-century work at the back. Wickens, which by 1664 was owned by the Dering family, seems to have been tenanted and contained six fireplaces, four of which are the fine sixteenth-century examples mentioned above (Fig. 7.16). Elsewhere in the rural parts of the parish large farmhouses tended to have three or four hearths and smaller houses had one or two. Few occupiers in the tax list can be correlated with surviving buildings, but one who can is Anthony Baldock, yeoman, who lived at Little Swan Street Farmhouse (Fig. 7.20), a smaller dwelling than the medieval Swan Street Farmhouse across the road. The house, which was originally timber-framed, with two rooms to the right of the stack, was built in the sixteenth century when it was served by a timber chimney, but by 1664 it had been upgraded and Baldock was charged on two hearths, which examination of the house shows heated the hall and the chamber over it. The left end of the house is later.

In 'Charing Towne', eleven of the fifty-six householders listed had four or more hearths. These included Mr Gabriel Peirce, by then the owner of 33 High Street to which he gave

Fig. 7.18 26, 28 High Street. No 26 (Ridgemount) is a former medieval open hall and service end of Wealden form. No 28 (Hope Haven) was rebuilt as a cross wing in the early seventeenth century (S Pearson)

Fig. 7.19 58, 60, 62 High Street (Elizabethan Court, formerly The Swan Inn). By the seventeenth century this was probably the largest inn in Charing (S Pearson)

his name, who was charged on eight hearths, and Mr Henry Ridgway, the vicar, who was charged on six. There was only one other gentleman in the town, but some of the traders also lived in large, albeit unidentified, houses, as indicated by their surviving probate inventories. Widow Burwish [sic] with six hearths was almost certainly the widow of a wealthy grocer Alexander Burwash, who had died in 1662. Richard Rade, butcher, whose probate inventory of 1683 indicates a house of eight rooms, was charged on four hearths. However, some traders were less well-off. Thomas Kilham, a fellmonger (dealer in hides and skins), was only charged on a single hearth. Surviving title deeds indicate that his son William lived at 30 High Street (Fig. 7.7, Map 2.13) and it is probable that he inherited this property from his father. The house itself was small and built in the early sixteenth century (see above), and the probate inventory taken at Thomas's death in 1674 suggests that it had been little altered. It had a hall with a chamber over, to one end of which was a shop at the front with a buttery behind it and a chamber above.

Twenty people with one or two hearths, and two with three, were exempted from paying the hearth tax. They included twelve women, almost all widows, who presumably lived alone. What kind of dwellings they occupied is not easy to ascertain, although Mr Gabriel Peirce's inventory of 1670 lists one or two items 'in the outhouses where Ms Wolfe and Sarah Harte live', implying that some accommodation for poor villagers may have been very makeshift. There is some evidence in the parish registers to suggest that at least by the 1690s the population, which had been stagnant throughout the seventeenth century, was beginning to increase. This would have put pressure on the existing housing stock and probably some of the larger houses which are in several occupations today had started to be divided by c.1700.

Fig. 7 20 Little Swan Street Farmhouse. A timber-framed house of the sixteenth century, later clad in brick. It had two fireplaces in 1664 (S Pearson)

Fear of witches

During the later sixteenth and early seventeenth centuries, fear of witches was widespread in Kent. None were identified in Charing, but in 1574 a young girl in the neighbouring parish of Westwell was accused of witchcraft, and between 1565 and 1657 thirteen of the many women who were tried for witchcraft at Maidstone assizes were hanged. Educated people tended to dismiss the claims as superstition, but ordinary folk were anxious and took precautions to protect themselves with counter-spells, most of which involved placing items in the chimney or under door sills, openings through which it was thought a witch might enter the house. Sporadic evidence for this practice has been found across Kent, but in Charing, thanks to the vigilance of Pat Winzar, three houses have been shown to have had objects associated with the fear of witches deposited, discovered when the houses were being renovated. At The Old

Fig. 7.21 The bellarmine jug found in the hearth of The Old House, Station Road (K DaSilva-Hill)

Fig. 7.22 Pett Place (J Grebby)

House, Station Road (Fig. 7.17, Map 2.22), a bellarmine jug or bottle (stoneware and salt-glazed with an image stamped on it), was found under the hearth of the seventeenth-century fireplace (Fig. 7.21). Such jugs were common in English taverns and alehouses and, filled with various items acting as counter-spells, were often used as 'witch bottles'. Two more were discovered under the hearths of the large chimney inserted at 29 High Street (Fig 7.12) when it was turned into a dwelling during the seventeenth century. In this instance the contents of one were examined and found to include objects such as hair, bent pins, powdered bone and pieces of pierced wood. At 32 High Street, an iron nail, wrapped in glued paper and with a linen tassel attached, had been set in wet mortar about 5ft (1.5m) up the chimney. All these were probably witch charms. At 52, 54 High Street (Hogben's), a number of seventeenth-century shoes walled up next to the chimney were not necessarily directly related to witch protection, although they were probably associated with other superstitions. The unusual number of such items found in Charing is entirely due to the watchful eye of Pat Winzar over many years, and suggests how common the practice of depositing items providing protection probably was.

Fig. 7.23 Wakeley House, High Street (S Pearson)

The eighteenth century and afterwards

The grandest house in the parish was undoubtedly Pett Place, by now in the hands of the Sayer family, who encased the earlier timber ranges and gave the house a particularly fine symmetrical brick façade of nine bays articulated by wide pilaster strips (Fig. 7.22). The probate inventory of George Sayer, who died in 1718, describes the contents of Pett at the time: there were about twenty rooms in all. Among other items the hall contained a 'Dutch' hearth for burning wood, a print of King George and a pendulum clock. The great parlour had a marble fireplace with a glass above lit by six glass sconces for candles, and was furnished with damask curtains, velvet covered chairs, and a pendulum clock. The dining room had fourteen 'caney' chairs, many pictures on the walls and a six-leaf Indian fire screen; and the best bedroom had tapestry hangings, bed curtains of damask, chairs covered with silver 'stuff', and landscapes on the walls. This was a house of considerable pretension.

Fig. 7.24 14, 16, High Street (S Pearson)

Fig. 7.25 29, 31, 33, 35 Station Road.
Weatherboarded cottages (S Pearson)

In the early eighteenth century Charing High Street received some fine brick houses. The earliest was Wakeley House (Fig. 7.23, Map 2.41) at the top end of the street, a double-pile house with a symmetrical façade set above a basement with attic rooms in the hipped roof. The central entry opened into the stair hall and there were two large rooms to both front and back. The quality of the cut and rubbed brickwork is quite different to the cruder brickwork of the seventeenth century. Ludwell House (Fig. 3.5, Map 2.39), further down the street, is not dissimilar. Another smart, although somewhat smaller house, built later in the century, is 17 High Street (Peckwater House, Map 2.32). Several plainer brick houses were also erected later in the century. At the north end of the street 64, 66 High Street (Old School House; Map 2.7) probably began life as two cottages, being turned into a school following a bequest by Elizabeth Ludwell in 1765, and remaining as such until the new school was built in 1872. Other examples are 68 High Street (Wheler House; Map 2.6), 80, 82 High Street and the Old Forge (Fig. 4.3, Map 2.5), the latter operating as a forge into the early twentieth century. At the bottom of the town, 14, 16 High Street was built as a single dwelling and later subdivided (Fig. 7.24, Map 2.19) Across the A20, three blocks of fine weatherboarded cottages remain at 29, 31, 33, 35 Station Road (Fig. 7.25, Map 2.24), the two outer ones each a single cottage with symmetrical facades, the central one built as a semidetached pair. Several good brick or brick and stone farmhouses were built to the north of the town, on the Downs, including Vent House (Fig. 7.26), Stalisfield Road and Stonestile, Stonestile Farm Road.

Fig. 7.26 Vent House, Stalisfield Road (S Pearson)

The nineteenth century likewise saw many changes. The parsonage, The Moat, by now owned by the Barwick family, was completely done over in the Gothick style, disguising the medieval Wealden hall house which remained inside. This was illustrated in several drawings and watercolours by Horace Barwick and others during the 1830s and 40s (Fig. 7.27, Map 2.16). These are among drawings forming the Hutton Collection, and one of them, illustrated as Figure 7.28, clearly highlights the kind of alterations that have taken place in the village over the last 150 years: Wakeley Villas, the brick cottages with Dutch gables next to Wakeley House (Map 2.42), have replaced a medieval building which still existed in the 1830s; and the sixteenth-century King's Head Inn (Map 2.40), which had an eighteenth-century front at that time, was refronted again in the early twentieth century when, among other things, the ground floor over the cellar was lowered to street level (Fig.7.29). To avoid winter flooding from an underground stream, many of the earlier houses in the High Street had raised ground floors over semi-sunken cellars, as can be seen in Figures 7.19 and 7.23.

Buildings other than houses also survive from the nineteenth century. On top of the hill is the early nineteenth-century smock mill (Fig. 4.4). In 1873, the new school was built in what now became School Road (Fig. 4.5), and in 1874, as Charing Heath began to expand as a separate settlement a new stone-built church was erected on a corner of the heath (Fig. 4.10). In Charing itself, the railway arrived in 1884 and the new station was built in the style of other stations along the route with patterned brickwork and a slate tiled roof (Fig.4.9), while the parish hall was built in 1897 (Fig. 4.11).

Charing is not particularly unusual in this part of Kent for the number and diversity of its historic buildings, but it is nonetheless an excellent parish in which to study what houses were like and how they changed between the Middle Ages and the twentieth century. Many medieval timber-framed houses in Kent were so well-built that there was little point in pulling them down and replacing them. Spacious dwellings in the rural areas, erected as working farmhouses in the fifteenth century, have now become fine country residences for those no longer engaged in farming. In the village, where tradesmen must always have predominated, similar if somewhat smaller houses remain, albeit rather more altered and

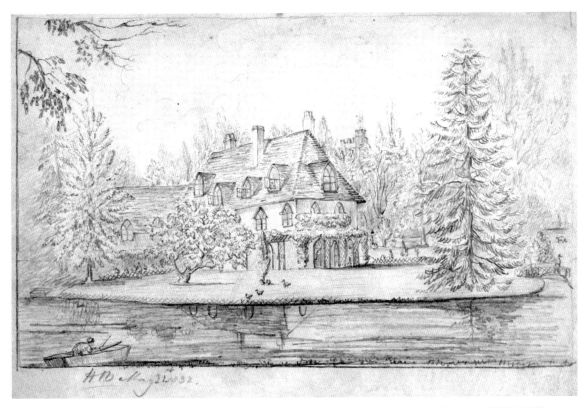

Fig. 7.27 The Moat, formerly Charing Rectory; drawn by Horace Barwick, 1832 (CDLHS)

*Fig. 7.28 The King's Head, Wakeley House and Wakeley Villas, High Street in the 1830s
(CDLHS)*

often divided into two or more dwellings. In most cases the timber-framed exteriors have been stuccoed, weatherboarded or clad in brick, and the timber-framed interiors are hidden from view. Although the overwhelming impression of Charing today is of brick and plaster, the steep and uneven roofs and overhanging first floors often indicate older origins. To these must be added the new, solid, brick dwellings of the eighteenth and nineteenth centuries, built when Charing was clearly a prosperous trading community serving a wide rural area. Throughout this time the centre remained much the same size, and it was only during the twentieth-century that the village expanded and new estates began to be added to the earlier core. This chapter has been concerned with what was built during the 500 years between 1400 and 1900, concentrating in particular on the many houses of the earlier part of the period that still stand today, hidden behind later facades.

Fig. 7.29 The former King's Head and Wakeley House in 2011 (S Dray)

Epilogue: Charing after 1900

by Brian Easton

In this collection of essays the writers have sought to describe the evolution of Charing from earliest prehistoric times up until the end of the nineteenth century. During that time the area now known as Charing progressed from an ice covered wilderness through early settlement to being a thriving village of some nineteen hundred souls, and the pace of development, particularly in the nineteenth century, is clearly evident. At the beginning of the nineteenth century there was severe depression, unemployment, and abject poverty. By the end of the century there were signs of real hope; communications had improved dramatically with the arrival of the railway and the telegraph giving access to markets and employment beyond the confines of the village and its immediate surroundings. The manufacture and distribution of gas brought significant benefits to the wealthier households and the introduction of mechanized farm machinery began to transform agriculture.

But all this pales into insignificance when set against the changes that were about to engulf the village in the twentieth century. The events of that single century would occupy another book at least as long as this one but that is no reason not to take a brief look at what was to come. It has been pointed out that generally the families with any influence that lived in the village in the late Middle Ages were not politically minded and so, up until the end of the nineteenth century, the inhabitants of Charing were not touched in their daily lives by events of international importance; but all this was to change with the outbreak of the Great War of 1914-18. A total of forty-two men from Charing lost their lives and of these, three were from the same family and two other families lost two members. Two Victoria Crosses were won by men who originated from Charing. It is interesting to note, however, that when Harry Ward, who was born in Charing in 1864 and lived all his life here, wrote his recollections of his early life in Charing, he never mentioned the First World War. So it would seem that although many families were touched by loss, the war itself did not have a direct impact on village life.

The Second World War certainly did have an impact. Charing was right at the centre of the area covered by the Battle of Britain; many recall watching the dog fights in the skies above Kent and visiting the sites of crashed German aircraft. The village was fortunate to avoid damage from bomb attack although the surrounding area did not go unscathed. A number of V1 flying bombs and V2 rockets were brought down or fell in the area, sometimes causing great damage and loss of life. In August 1944 a V1 was brought down by gunfire and crashed on Little Chart church, demolishing it completely except for the tower; the ruins of which have been preserved and can be seen to this day. Even more tragic was the V1 which was shot down on the 24 June 1944 and fell on Newlands farm where a Royal Electrical and Mechanical Engineers detachment of the 6th Guards Tank Brigade were assembled for embarkation to Normandy two days later. Fifty-two REME personnel were killed of whom forty-six are buried in Lenham cemetery and six elsewhere. This was the largest single loss of life suffered by the REME Corps and a truly great tragedy.

As the war swung from a defensive to an offensive operation Charing found itself at the centre of the preparations for the D-day landings. In the spring of 1943, the 9th Battalion Royal Tank Regiment arrived from Gateshead and was quartered in and around Charing. Their headquarters were at Pett Place and the tanks and men were dispersed around the village at Longbeech, Stalisfield, and Hall's Place. They embarked for France at Gosport on the 19 June 1944, so for more than a year Charing was at the heart of a very significant part of the war effort. A memorial to the dead of the 9th Battalion was placed on the south wall of the nave in the church and their comrades who survived the war visited Charing, with their spouses, for a short service and reunion on the anniversary of D-Day every year until 2010.

An area greatly affected by change in the twentieth century was agriculture, and Charing, which was predominantly an arable farming area, was in the forefront of change. In Chapter 4 we read that in 1827 farm labourers began to vent their resentment at the introduction of the threshing machine, believing that they were losing work as a result. By the 1940s, the threshing machine was an established piece of farm machinery seen in practically every farmyard in late winter, noisily separating the grain from the straw. But it still needed a group of at least three or more men to manage the operation. By the end of the century farmers had replaced the traditional five-barred gate with a double width metal one to allow the monster combine harvester onto their fields which in one operation cut and thrashed the grain and delivered it by the ton into a trailer drawn by a multi-horsepower tractor. The whole operation needed just two men.

Perhaps the most dramatic and influential area of change was in the field of communications, on land, sea and in the air. At the beginning of the twentieth century manned flight was in its infancy with fragile aircraft made of wood, wire, and silk taking wobbly to the air. By the time of the Second World War fighting aircraft were a significant element in the planning of a war campaign and the establishment of air superiority became a major part of strategy. The technology developed under the pressure of war spilled over into civil aviation and in less than fifty years the contrails of Battle of Britain fighters in the blue skies above Charing had been succeeded by those at 30,000ft of huge airliners carrying as many as 600 or more passengers half way round the world.

The development of the internal combustion engine had a similar effect on land transport and in Charing this led, in the 1920s, to changing the course of the A20 and building the A252 to Canterbury across the old Westfield including the fair field. This meant that Canterbury and Ashford traffic could avoid the High Street. A new section of the A20 was built cutting across the southern end of the High Street which involved the demolition of the Queen's Head Inn and several houses on either side and opposite it. The inn was rebuilt nearby but facing the new road and a cross roads was created. This provided some relief for a few decades, but the inevitable growth of motor traffic nationally led to the introduction of motorways, and so the M20 to the south of the village was opened in 1991. This had an immediate and beneficial effect on the amount of traffic passing through on the A20.

The building of the Channel Tunnel in the 1980s presaged the need for a rail system carrying trains which could reach speeds of 186 miles per hour. In the late eighties rumours were rife that a new high speed rail line would actually run alongside the existing line, just south of the A20 and demolishing several houses. The citizens of Charing were up-in-arms and showed their united opposition to this plan in a demonstration march in Maidstone in

1989. A long period of review and revision ensued and it was another fourteen years before the Channel Tunnel Rail Link finally opened with a section running through the parish but a mile south of Charing village. The building of the line led to very significant archaeological finds along the excavated route and these are still being recorded and assessed.

Thus in a century Charing had come from being a relatively secluded Victorian village supported by agriculture and associated trades to one opened up to the wide world with high speed road and rail links to London and the rest of the country and to Europe and beyond. But these advances have their negative sides. Many of the trades seen on the High Street at the end of the nineteenth century have disappeared and not been replaced. Premises have been converted to domestic dwellings. Property values have escalated making it difficult for the younger generation to remain as residents in the village. The same is true of the farmhouses and cottages in the rural areas, which have largely ceased to function as such. Many of the houses in the village and in the outlying areas have become homes to 'incomers': people retiring from lives elsewhere, or professionals taking advantage of the ability to live in a beautiful rural setting and yet use the high speed communications to travel to work in London or some other distant centre of business. Even so at the end of the twentieth century Charing still had a post office, two general stores, two butchers, an ironmonger, a greengrocer and florist, a newsagent, a watchmaker, a hairdresser and an estate agent. By the end of the first decade of the twenty-first century the ironmonger, the greengrocer and florist, the watchmaker and the dedicated newsagent had gone and not been replaced, although papers can still be bought in several village outlets.

Underlying all these developments has been a quite dramatic increase in the population of the village and parish, particularly after World War 2. In 1664 the parish was recorded as having just 170 households. By the end of the nineteenth century there were 300; it had not even doubled in just under 250 years. But by 1999 there were 1180 dwellings; 700 centred on the village and approach roads, 100 in Charing Heath and thirty in Westwell Leacon, which was added to the parish in the 1950s. The relatively unchanging nucleus around the village centre has been gradually expanded by the addition of a number of new estates and small groups of houses.

The pace of change seems inexorable but if a resident at the end of the nineteenth century could be brought back now they would still recognise the village. Although they would see that a significant number of new houses have been built in a variety of locations; that a modern fire station has been built and a modern library erected on the site of an old slaughterhouse, other features remain. The school is still there, albeit with a modern extension, the church and archbishop's palace are virtually unchanged from a century ago, Clewards survives, now officially designated a village green, most of the old farmhouses remain, and the heart of the parish, its residents, are still welcoming and deeply appreciative of the wonderful piece of Kent history in which they are privileged to live, knowing that it is theirs for a season to pass on to their successors, changed but unchanging.

Further Reading

The books and articles listed below are those which the authors feel may be of most interest to readers who wish to find out more about aspects of the parish or the history of Kent. In addition, it will be clear from the text that a great deal of detail has been obtained directly from primary sources; these are mainly to be found in the archives of the Centre for Kentish Studies, Maidstone, the Canterbury Cathedral Archives, and the National Archives, Kew. Many of the documents used have been transcribed by Pat Winzar, and the transcriptions are in her private possession or held in the archives of the Charing and District Local History Society.

Earlier articles about aspects of Charing's history were published in Charing and District Local History Society, *About Charing: Town and Parish* (Kent County Council, 1984).

Chapter 1: Charing before the Norman Conquest

S Brookes and S Harrington, *The Kingdom and People of Kent, AD 400-1066* (Stroud: The History Press, 2010).

N Brooks, *The Early History of the Church of Canterbury* (Leicester University Press, 1984).

A P Detsicas, 'A Romano-British Building at Charing', *Archaeologia Cantiana,* vol. 91 (1975), pp. 107-10.

A P Detsicas, *The Cantiaci* (Gloucester: Alan Sutton 1983).

A Everitt, *Continuity and Colonization: the Evolution of Kentish Settlement* (Leicester University Press, 1986).

Kent County Council, Charing parish in 'Exploring Kent's Past': http://www.kent.gov.uk// ExploringKentsPast

P Kidson, 'A metrological investigation,' *Journal of the Warburg and Courtauld Institutes*, vol 53 (1990) pp. 71-97.

J H Williams (ed.), *The Archaeology of Kent to AD 800* (Kent County Council, 2007), various articles.

K P Witney, *The Jutish Forest: A Study of the Weald of Kent from 450 to 1380 AD* (University of London, Athlone Press, 1976).

Chapter 2: Medieval Charing

R Eales, 'Introduction' to *The Kent Domesday'* (London: Alecto Historical Editions, 1992).

F R H Du Boulay, *The Lordship of Canterbury* (London: Nelson, 1966).

E Hasted, *The History and Topographical Survey of the County of Kent*, vol. 7 (1799, 2nd edn reprint 1972), pp. 429-48.

M Mate, 'The economy of Kent' in S Sweetinburgh (ed.), *Later Medieval Kent, 1220-1540* (Kent County Council, Boydell Press, 2010), pp. 1-24.

P M Winzar, 'Eversley – a 13th century estate', in Charing and District Local History Society, *About Charing* (Kent County Council, 1984), pp. 17-19.

P M Winzar, 'Peirce House, Charing: the house and its owners', *Archaeologia Cantiana*, vol. 111 (1993), pp. 131-200.

K P Witney (ed.), *The Survey of Archbishop Pecham's Kentish Manors, 1283-85*, Kent Records, vol. 28 (Kent Archaeological Society, 2000).

Chapter 3: Early Modern Charing

A Armstrong (ed.), *The Economy of Kent, 1640-1914* (Kent County Council, Boydell Press, 1995), various articles.

C W Chalklin, *Seventeenth Century Kent* (London: Longmans, 1965).

P Clark, *English Provincial Society from the Reformation to the Civil War: Religion and Politics in Kent, 1500-1640* (Hassocks: Harvester Press, 1977).

Dictionary of National Biography: articles on 'Sir Edward Dering'; 'Mary Honywood'; 'Sir Robert Honywood [the younger]'; 'Sir George Wheler'.

A Everitt, *The Community of Kent and the Great Rebellion, 1640-60* (Leicester University Press, 1966).

F Lansberry (ed.), *Government and Politics in Kent, 1640-1914* (Kent County Council, Boydell Press, 2001), various articles.

N Yates, R Hume and P Hastings, *Religion and Society in Kent, 1640-1914* (Kent County Council: Boydell Press, 1994),

P M Winzar, 'Charing Town: traders and craftsmen of the seventeenth century', unpublished Dip. Loc. Hist. thesis (University of Kent, Canterbury, 1982).

M Zell (ed.), *Early Modern Kent, 1540-1640* (Kent County Council, Boydell Press, 2000), various articles.

Chapter 4: Charing in the nineteenth century

A Armstrong (ed.), *The Economy of Kent, 1640-1914* (Kent County Council, Boydell Press, 1995), various articles.

S Bagshaw, *Charing School, 1873-1973* (Kent County Council, 1973).

E Higgs, *Making Sense of the Census Revisited* (London: Institute of Historical Research, 2005).

F Lansberry (ed.), *Government and Politics in Kent 1640-1914* (Kent County Council, Boydell Press, 2001), various articles.

W Page (ed.), *Victoria History of the County of Kent*, vol. 3 (London: Dawsons, reprint 1974).

H Ward, *My Early Recollections of Charing since 1868* (Charing and District Local History Society, 2002).

R T Wyllie, 'Holy Trinity Church, Charing Heath: historical notes', unpublished typescript held in the vestry (1985).

N Yates, R Hume and P Hastings, *Religion and Society in Kent 1640-1914* (Kent County Council, Boydell Press, 1994), various articles.

Chapter 5: The church of St Peter and St Paul

C Currie, 'Furniture and Woodwork in the Churchwardens' Accounts, Charing, Kent, 1590-1635', *Regional Furniture History*, vol. 21 (2007), pp. 95-112.

D R Fotheringham, *Historic Charing* (Charing: John Moody, 3rd edn, 1936).

S Glynne, *Notes on the Churches of Kent* (London: John Murray, 1854).

L R A Grove, 'The Church of St Peter and St Paul', in Charing and District Local History Society, *About Charing* (Kent County Council, 1984), pp. 5-13.

A. Hussey, *Notes on the Churches in the Counties of Kent, Sussex and Surrey mentioned in the Domesday Book* (London: John Russell Smith, 1852).

J C L Stahlschmidt, *The Church Bells of Kent* (London: E. Stock, 1887).

C H K Williams, 'Charing clocks, clockmakers and clock-keepers', *Archaeologia Cantiana*, vol. 125 (2005), pp. 183-202; vol. 126 (2006), pp. 87-114.

Chapter 6: The Archbishop's Palace

S Pearson, 'The archbishop's palace at Charing in the Middle Ages', *Archaeologia Cantiana*, vol. 121 (2001), pp. 315-49. Many other sources are cited there.

George Wheler, 'Notes on the life of Sir George Wheler, knight', *The Genealogist*, NS vol. 2 (1885), pp. 202-11, vol. 3 (1886), pp. 41-9, 216-20.

Chapter 7: Historic houses of Charing

D Harrington, S Pearson, S Rose (eds), *Kent Hearth Tax Assessment, Lady Day 1664* (British Record Society, Hearth Tax Series 2, 2000).

P S Barnwell and A T Adams, *The House Within: Interpreting Medieval Houses in Kent* (Royal Commission on the Historical Monuments of England/Her Majesty's Stationery Office, 1994).

S Pearson, *The Medieval Houses of Kent: An Historical Analysis* (Royal Commission on the Historical Monuments of England/Her Majesty's Stationery Office, 1994).

S Pearson, P S Barnwell and A T Adams, *A Gazetteer of Medieval Houses in Kent* (Royal Commission on the Historical Monuments of England/Her Majesty's Stationery Office, 1994).

P M Winzar, 'Witchcraft and counter-spells in Charing', *Archaeologia Cantiana*, vol. 115 (1995), pp. 23-8.

Index

Page numbers in bold type indicate the location of figures or tables

List of buildings marked on Map 2